Introduction to Picture Interpretation

According to C.G. Jung

Theodor Abt

LIVING HUMAN HERITAGE PUBLICATIONS, ZURICH

Studies from the

RESEARCH AND TRAINING CENTRE
FOR DEPTH PSYCHOLOGY
ACCORDING TO C.G. JUNG AND MARIE-LOUISE VON FRANZ

Introduction to Picture Interpretation

According to C.G. Jung

Theodor Abt

LIVING HUMAN HERITAGE PUBLICATIONS, ZURICH
2005

Second edition 2019
First edition 2005
Living Human Heritage Publications
Münsterhof 16, 8001 Zurich, Switzerland
info@livinghumanheritage.org
www.livinghumanheritage.org

ISBN 3-9522608-2-7

Copyright © 2005 by Theodor Abt
All rights reserved including the right of reproduction
in whole or in part, in any form.

Edited by Frith Luton

FRONTCOVER: Picture by a 32-year-old European woman

LAYOUT: S. Neşe Coşkun, Ediz Çalışkan and Theodor Abt

COLOUR SEPARATION, PRINTING AND BINDING:
MAS MATBAACILIK A.Ş. ISTANBUL

Contents

Foreword	9
Introduction—The Discovery of the Unconscious	11
Part 1—Need for an Approach to Picture Interpretation According to C.G. Jung	**13**
1.1. In the Beginning was the Image	15
1.2. Word and Image	17
1.3. Instinct and Image	20
1.4. Universal Patterns of Imagination	25
1.5. Archetype and Symbol	27
1.6. Images as Bridges to the Unconscious	29
1.7. Effects of Pictures	33
Part 2—Proposal for a Method in Picture Interpretation	**39**
2.1. Interpretation as «The Art of Creating Consciousness»	41
a. The Two Attitudes	42
b. The Four Functions of Consciousness	44
2.2. A Possible Way to Proceed	46
a. Circumambulation with the Four Functions	46
b. The Hypothesis and its Opposite	47
c. From the «Living Cell» to the Interpretation	49
2.3. Dangers of Interpretation	52
2.4. Analysis and Synthesis	54
Part 3—Tools for Interpretation	**57**
3.1. Associations and Amplifications	59
3.2. Amplification of Material Aspects	61
a. Sheet	61
b. Medium	62
c. Frame	67
d. Format	67
3.3. Formal Aspects	69
a. Organization	69
b. Proportion	71
c. Movement	74

3.4. Space Symbolism	76
a. The Quality of Location	76
b. Perspective	80
3.5. Colour Symbolism	84
a. Basic Aspects	84
b. The Three Basic Colours (Red, Blue, Yellow)	90
c. The Three Basic Mixed Colours (Green, Orange, Violet)	96
d. Other Colours and Non-Colours (Brown, Black, Grey, White)	102
e. Mixed Colours in General	108
3.6. Number Symbolism	109
a. The Symbolic Nature of Numbers	109
b. Numbers as Basic Elements of Order	113
c. Amplification of the First Ten Numbers	116
Number 1	116
Number 2	120
Number 3	123
Number 4	127
Number 5	131
Number 6	138
Number 7	141
Number 8	147
Number 9	148
Number 10	152
d. Numbers from 11 to 17	155
Number 11	155
Number 12	156
Number 13	160
Number 14	162
Number 15	163
Number 16	164
Number 17	165
3.7. Motifs	166
3.8. Potential Criteria for Latent Psychosis	169
Part 4—Some Final Considerations	**173**
Bibliography	177
Index	181
Sources of the Pictures	194

«It is as if something somewhere were 'known' in the form of images—but not by us.»

Marie-Louise von Franz,
C.G. Jung, His Myth in Our Time, p. 240

Foreword

This guidebook is the result of my teaching picture interpretation at the C.G. Jung Institute in Zurich-Küsnacht 1977–1994 and, since 1995, at the Research and Training Centre in Depth Psychology according to C.G. Jung and Marie-Louise von Franz in Zurich, Switzerland.

My teacher in picture interpretation was Dr Rudolf Michel, the first curator of the picture-archive of the C.G. Jung Institute. After his early death in 1976, I was asked by the Curatorium of the C.G. Jung Institute to take over the training for the English-speaking students. At that time, the method of picture interpretation—according to the psychology of C.G. Jung—was mainly based on Jolande Jacobi's German book *«Vom Bilderreich der Seele, Wege und Umwege zu sich selbst»*, which came out in 1963. Rudolf Michel had been asked by a publisher to write a comparable book on picture interpretation in English. Soon after starting to teach at the Jung Institute, I was asked by this publisher whether I could write that book. The offer was tempting. But I realised that my approach to understanding pictures had not reached maturity and lacked my personal foundation. I felt the need to find my own way of allowing the pictures from the unconscious to reveal their meaning or, in other words, to enable them to start speaking.

It initially needed intensive studies in alchemy for me to realize that the process of working out the meaning of a picture is basically a process of «distilling out gold», «the gold of the sages» as the old masters of alchemy used to call it, namely consciousness. In the same way as in the work of the alchemist, «gold» or conscious understanding of a picture cannot be obtained without broad experience, disciplined method and great dedication with regard to the mystery enshrined in the object of study. The method proposed here grew and developed thanks to the dialogue with students in my lectures, seminars and especially control-case colloquia. It is born out of practice and meant as an aid for practice. This book is an attempt to show *how to illuminate a picture with its own light,* as Marie-Louise von Franz once put it. On the other hand, we shall also see how to best avoid prejudice arising from our own fixed ideas as to what a picture should mean. My own guideline for picture interpretation is the respectful and unprejudiced approach of C. G. Jung to the reality of the objective psyche. He speaks of the *objective psyche* in order to point out that there is some independent 'other' in us that expresses itself in images. These appear mainly in dreams, fantasies, visions and active imaginations.

The reproduction of most pictures in this book is possible thanks to the generous permission of the people I had the opportunity to work with in analysis. We will mainly seek to understand some aspects of these pictures from the unconscious. Whether they are to be considered as art or not is not relevant here.

The chapter on number symbolism is based on a lecture series given at the C.G. Jung Institute in the Summer Semester of 1985. It came out in a private edition in 1988. Dr Marie-Louise von Franz was kind enough to look through that manuscript.

A future volume will include examples illustrating how the application of the method presented here allows us to make pictures from the past (rock-art, alchemical visions etc.) and from the present reveal some of their inner meaning and thus somehow become alive.

I would like to thank Joyce Bogusky, Dr Richard Chachère, Susanne Doebel, Tom Elsner, Stan Fineman, Dr Ruedi Högger, Frith Luton, Sabine Mayer-Patzel, Dr Nikola Patzel, Jean Palmer-Daley, Colette Rizzo, David Roscoe, Dr Peter Starr and Katya Walter for their cooperation in ensuring that this book could be produced. A warm «thank you» also goes to Istanbul to S. Neşe Coşkun and Ediz Çalışkan for the layout and to Ufuk N. Şahin and Mehmet Bora Akgül for the printing and good supervision, as well as to all the students who attended my lectures, seminars and control-case colloquia. They contributed with their questions, criticisms and suggestions. My deep gratitude goes to Marie-Louise von Franz who accompanied and supported my search for a better understanding of pictures until her death in 1998. Without her, this book would not have been possible. Last but not least I thank my wife Regina, who at all times supported and encouraged me in my research.

Zurich, Autumn 2004   Theodor Abt

Introduction
The Discovery of the Unconscious

The breakthrough in the development of modern depth psychology came right at the beginning of the last century in 1900. At the time when the physicist Max Planck discovered a new model for understanding external nature—the quantum theory—, Sigmund Freud discovered a new reality of our inner nature. He called this part of our psyche the *subconscious*. He concluded that this realm is a secondary phenomenon to consciousness, its «garbage can» so to speak, filled with repressed wishes of the individual. Seeking insight into this reality, he discovered that dreams are an essential guide. He therefore called dreams the *«via regia»* (royal path) to the subconscious. His publication *«Traumdeutung»* marked a pivotal point in the development of modern depth psychology.[1]

Freud's book inspired the young psychiatrist Carl Gustav Jung, who then became one of the early supporters and followers of Freud's theory of the psyche. But Jung's personal experiences brought him to a different conclusion about this inner nature. He formulated the *hypothesis of the existence of a collective or common unconscious*. This means that there are not only psychic structures common to all human beings at all times, but also that this realm is an *independent second psychic system*, the origin of consciousness and basis of all creativity. Both facts are highly relevant for the interpretation of pictures emerging from the unconscious. The following diagram (Fig. 1) may be helpful in visualizing this concept of the psyche.

Furthermore, Jung was able to demonstrate that by studying and pondering over one's own images from the unconscious, one engages in a process of becoming more and more conscious of one's creative potential and unique meaning in life. He called this process *individuation*. The regulating centre, that by this process becomes more and more conscious, he named the *Self*.

---

[1] S. Freud, *The Interpretation of Dreams*.

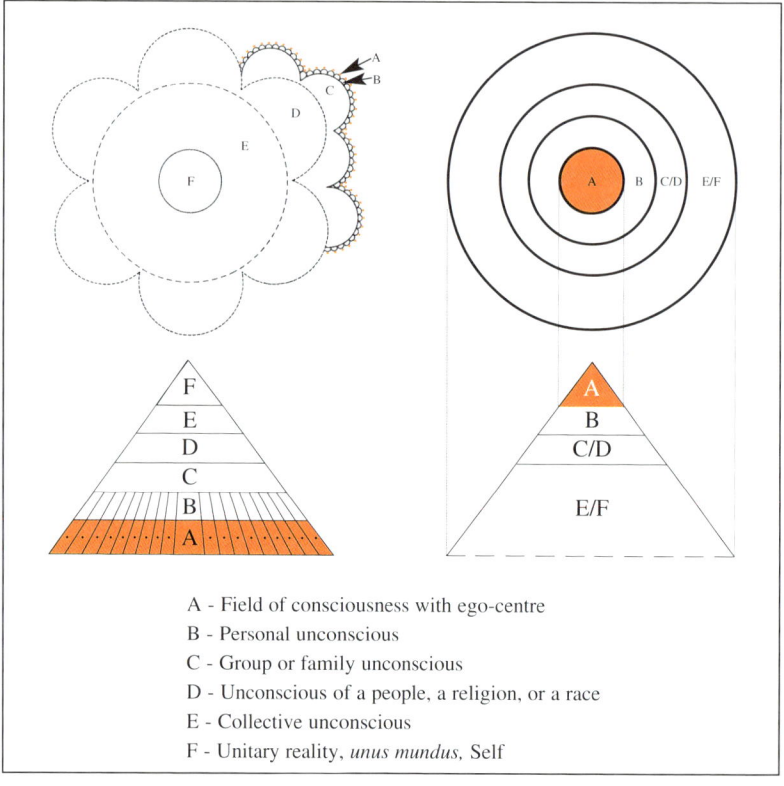

Fig. 1: Two complementary views of the structure of the psyche according to C.G. Jung[2]

Because the unconscious appears to us in dreams, fantasies, visions and active imaginations often in the form of images, it became crucial for Jung to understand the meaning of his own and his clients' pictures. He often advised people he worked with «to express themselves by pencil or brush. This procedure has proved to be most valuable, especially with people unable to express their fantasies verbally; in addition it enabled the patient to actively cooperate with the treatment in their spare time».[3] For these reasons, the art of picture interpretation became important in the training of Jungian analysts.

---

[2] M.-L. von Franz, *Projection and Recollection*, pp. 80–81. The left pyramid has been added by the author.

[3] E.A. Bennet, *Vorwort* in: C.G. Jung, *Das symbolische Leben* [GW 18/I], p. 18 (only in the German edition of the *Collected Works*).

Part 1

Need for an Approach to Picture Interpretation According to C.G. Jung

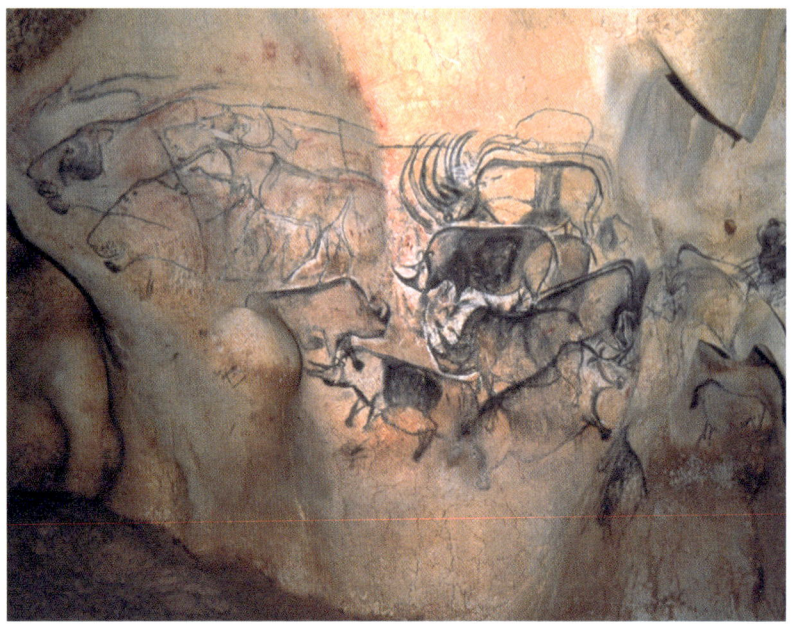

Fig. 2 and 3: Rock paintings from the cave of Chauvet, France; 32,000 years old.

1.1. In the Beginning was the Image

In order to develop an appropriate attitude towards picture interpretation, it is important to clarify certain basic concepts. What is an image? What is the function of images? Images have a primordial function for animals and humans. First of all, perception of the outer world—that is here the interpretation of all the impulses of the sense organs by the brain—occurs via images. The neurobiologist Gerald Hüther, in the course of his research concerning the power of images, speaks of this union of what is seen in the outer world overlaid with inner images, as the transformation of the outer image into a new, specific «see-image»; what is heard is transformed into a «hear-image», what is smelled becomes an inner «smell-image», what is touched an inner «touch-image».[1] If the emotional impact of these images is strong enough, they reach consciousness.

C.G. Jung himself wrote about the importance of images: «It is as if we did not know or else continuously forgot, that everything of which we are conscious is an image and image *is* psyche».[2] Indeed, we are often not aware of the fact that *whatever becomes conscious appears first as an image*. Jung used the word *image* simply in the sense of a representation. A psychic entity can be represented—and thus become a *conscious content*—only if it has the quality of an image. He therefore calls all conscious contents images, since they are reflections of processes in the brain.[3] He states that the psyche consists of reflected images, that is of simple processes in the brain and reproductions of an almost infinite series. These images have the quality of consciousness.[4] Thus images are, as will become obvious from this book, central to the *process of becoming conscious*.

As we can already see in rock art all over the world, even the first pictures of humans are not only the result of a representation of an outer perception and a consciously intended image. They can also express, to a certain degree, contents from the inner world, mirroring what is *momentarily*

---

[1] From G. Hüther, *Die Macht der inneren Bilder* (The Power of Inner Images), p. 22f.
[2] C.G. Jung, *Alchemical Studies* [Coll. Works 13], § 75.
[3] C.G. Jung, *Structure and Dynamics of the Psyche* [Coll. Works 8], § 608.
[4] C.G. Jung, *Structure and Dynamics of the Psyche* [Coll. Works 8], § 610.

constellated in the unconscious. By drawing and painting such images, humans gradually became conscious of representations from the inner world and could share with others what originated from the unconscious. As far as one can register and represent what comes up from the unconscious realm, one is able to bring the spirit of the unconscious into consciousness. This ability marks the *dawn of the human spirit*.[5]

The following rock painting (Fig. 4) is one of the earliest representations of such an experience of something spiritual from the inner world entering human consciousness. It is the so-called birdman of Lascaux, a prehistoric cave in western France, and dating back approximately 17,000 years. The picture is found in a pit deep down in a cave and shows a human being with a bird's head. The idea of the birdman is found later in human civilisation again and again, for instance in ancient Egypt in the form of the god Thot, who is often represented by an Ibis-headed human. The birdman is the mediator between this world and the other world of the spirit, a messenger of the gods. This coming together of representations of the outer world (bird and man) and the inner realm of fantasy (birdman), as we can see in Lascaux, makes us aware that even in Neolithic times humans communicated about both worlds, the outer and the inner.

Fig. 4: The so-called birdman of Lascaux, a prehistoric cave in western France, dating back approximately 17,000 years.[6]

---

5   These thoughts were developed for an exhibition on rock art from all continents, called «The Dawn of the Human Spirit». It opened first in Cologne, Germany in 2000 under the title «*Am Anfang war das Bild*» and since then has travelled to major cities in Europe.

6   J. Clottes and D. Lewis-Williams, *Schamanen*, p. 36.

1.2. Word and Image

Archaic humans did not need to learn how to read pictures out of a book. Being able to read the «Book of Nature» was necessary for survival, however. This meant, for example, an uncanny ability to «read» animal-tracks, to find opportunities for hunting or to avoid danger; or a skill in «reading» the sky, predicting the weather or «reading» the body language of other humans or animals. We are all born with this ability to read pictures. All small children and their mothers understand each other with the help of body language that is simply a language of pictures. And every child also has a natural pleasure, urge and ability to draw and to paint.

But with the development and strengthening of ego-consciousness, especially with the general trends in education over the last two centuries, goal-oriented linear thinking has become the norm. The main subjects of learning today are reading, writing, grammar and mathematics. This training in linear thinking proved to be very successful for solving certain problems. Drawing and the original «thinking in images» became less important, counted little for promotion in school and were thus neglected. Today, in the Western world, linear thinking is the dominant way of adapting to the world. And the understanding of chains of cause and effect is the dominant way of looking at reality.

With this growing predominance of linear thinking during the last 200 years, the ability to read pictures has declined. Many people accordingly have lost faith in their ability to draw and paint. How often in my consultation hours have I heard the objection: «No way can I draw a picture of this dream motif, I just can't do that—I am not a painter». On the other hand, rarely does anyone hesitate to write down a dream or text, saying «I am not a writer».

The evolution of the two modes of perception is strongly linked to the development of consciousness in humans, which is, phylogenetically seen, again related to the growth of the cerebrum in human beings. We can, roughly speaking, say that this upper part of our brain, the phylogenetically youngest part of our «four brain-parts», is somehow related to the development of consciousness and the day world of ego-consciousness; whereas the three older parts of our brain, the limbic system, the brain stem as well as the so-called gut-brain[7] are parts that we basically have in common with our animal ancestors (see Fig. 5).

---

[7] Our gut is enerved by the enteric nervous system, which is considered as a complex integrative brain in its own right. See Michael D. Gershon, *The Second Brain*.

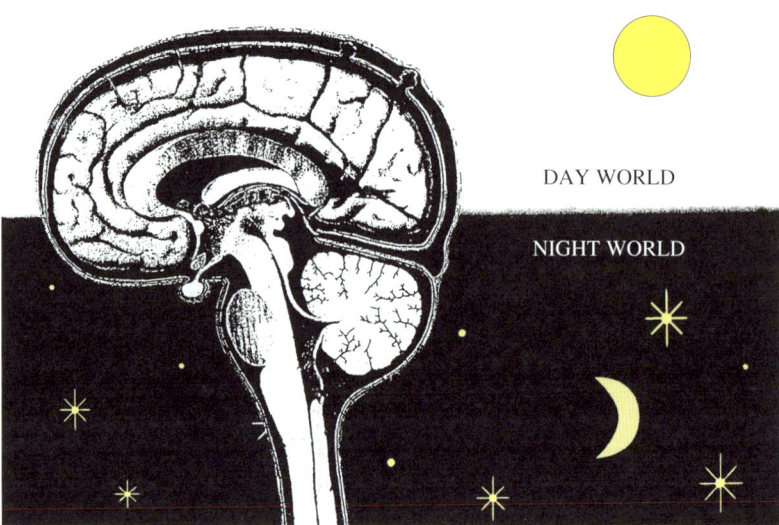

Fig. 5: This illustration symbolizes how the youngest, upper part of the brain is mainly connected to the day-world and to conscious functions while the older, lower parts of the brain are mainly connected to unconscious processes. But we have to remain aware that at night—of course—the whole brain structure is involved in the phases of dreaming.

While «image thinking» and linear thinking are related to the older and the younger parts of the brain respectively, there is also a corresponding specialization between the two cerebral hemispheres of the cortex, as modern brain research has made evident (Fig. 6). The two modes of perception—the linear and the image-spatial—are often connected with a stronger activity in one of the two hemispheres of our brain. Intensive research has shown that linear thinking usually activates mainly the left hemisphere, while with spatial and image thinking both hemispheres are active, with a dominance in the right hemisphere.[8] (The two hemispheres are connected by nerve bundles, called the *corpus callosum*.)

---

[8] Mainly based on the research of Roger W. Sperry, for which he received the Nobel prize in 1981.

[9] See for example G.M. Edelman and G. Tononi, *A Universe of Consciousness* and G. Hüther, *Die Welt der inneren Bilder*. Betty Edwards has written an excellent and helpful book, called *Drawing on the Right Side of the Brain,* about how to regain or liberate our drawing capacities. Step by step, one is shown how to learn to trust one's inborn ability to see and even to draw a portrait.

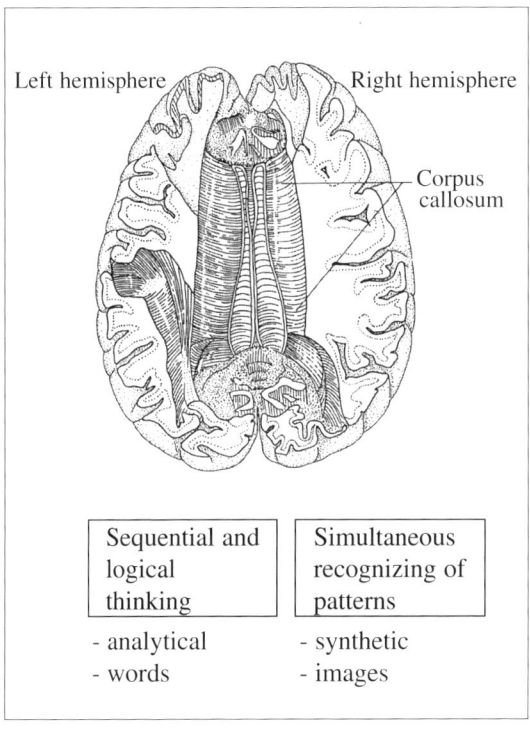

Fig. 6: The two hemispheres of the cerebrum and their predominant activity.

The research into the functioning of our brain is deeply fascinating[9] as the reality of the unconscious is also projected onto it. One could therefore speak to a certain extent of a modern brain mythology. Be it the right side of the cerebrum, be it the older parts of our brain; the unconscious can never be fixed and limited to a specific part of our body, as it is connected to all our bodily instincts.

In spite of all the evidence that there is a relationship between our psychic perception and the brain, it remains important to keep in mind that «the psychic is a phenomenal world in itself, *which can be reduced neither to the brain nor to metaphysics*».[10]

---

[10] See C.G. Jung, *Mysterium Coniunctionis*, [Coll. Works 14], § 673 (my italics).

1.3. Instinct and Image

In animals, instincts are mostly activated and restricted by images[11] which trigger off something from within. For example, the silhouette image of a bird of prey on a window will trigger off a flight reaction in small birds (see Fig. 7). Or when two male dogs, say Bobby and Bless, fight with each other and Bobby sees that he is going to lose the fight, he offers his neck to Bless. What does Bless now do? If he is not neurotic, Bobby's picture of submission will immediately stop Bless's aggressive drive; the meaning of the fight is now fulfilled, it has become clear which dog is the leader.

Fig. 7: Silhouettes of birds of prey, which here are marked with a "+", trigger a flight reaction in ducks and grey geese. Those silhouettes without "+" do not trigger such a reaction.[12]

---

[11] Zoologists use the word "trigger" for such images.
[12] See N. Tinbergen, *The Study of Instinct,* Chapter: "Behaviour as Reaction to External Stimuli-Sign Stimuli", p. 32.

Instincts are affiliated to trigger images, images in the sense as we saw before, including hear-images, smell-images and touch-images. Instincts define the pattern of behaviour in animals. At first glance, it seems that instinctual reactions are «all or nothing»: that once an urge is activated, it overrules any other urge. For example, a stag which pursues a hind in heat will not think of self-preservation and may be easy prey for a hunter. But even animals may behave flexibly in some situations, choosing between conflicting drives. For example, if danger threatens a brooding bird, it may at first choose to stay and protect its eggs (the reproduction instinct); but later, if the danger comes too close, the bird may suddenly fly away (the self-preservation instinct).

Instincts also strongly influence the behaviour of humans. In humans we find basic patterns of behaviour that we humans have in common with our animal ancestors. These patterns include, for example, self-assertion and reproduction. Each instinct is associated with certain images, which regulate its activity and give it its specific meaning and measure. When speaking of instinct in this book, I mean what is commonly understood by this word, «namely an *impulsion* (= drive) towards certain activities. The impulsion can come from an inner or outer stimulus which triggers off the mechanism of instinct psychically.»[13] Jung explains that «there are, in fact, no amorphous instincts, as every instinct bears in itself the pattern of its situation. Always it fulfils an image, and the image has fixed qualities. ... If any one of these conditions is lacking, the instinct does not function, because it cannot exist without its total pattern, without its image ... . We may say that the image represents the meaning of the instinct».[14]

Compared to animals, humans have a greater ability to control their urges and to differentiate their behaviour by choosing consciously, for they have a certain amount of psychic energy at their disposal, so-called free will. They have developed an ego-consciousness that enables them to make decisions in cases of conflicting drives. The psychologist Marie-Louise von Franz assumes that, as a result of evolution, human ego-consciousness emerged as a successful reconciliation between the imaginary counterparts of different instincts.[15] The cohesive force that holds these imaginary counterparts together is a property of consciousness.[16]

A testimony to this emerging ego-consciousness can be found in the innumerable hand drawings on rocks all over the world, some of them over 30,000 years old. They can be understood as expressing the realization: «Here I am in this world. I am!» In these drawings we can see another symbol of the *dawn of the human spirit* (Fig. 8 and 9).

---

[13] C.G. Jung, *Psychological Types* [Coll. Works 6], § 765, «Definitions».
[14] C.G. Jung, *Structure and Dynamics of the Psyche* [Coll. Works 8], § 398.
[15] M.-L. von Franz, *Patterns of Creativity Mirrored in Creation Myths*, p. 104f.
[16] C.G. Jung, *Structure and Dynamics of the Psyche* [Coll. Works 8], § 611.

Fig. 8: Hand stencils on rocks can be found all over the world. These are from Arnhem Land, in the Northern Territory of Australia.[17] They are an expression of «Here I am». This is the dawn of the human spirit.

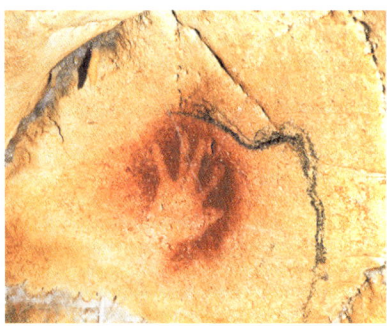

Fig. 9: Hand stencil from the cave of Chauvet, France; 32,000 years old.

The human psyche is, in the same way as the body, a self-regulating system. Instinct and image, drive-dynamism and spiritual (= meaningful) order are in a constant

---

[17] G. Chaloupka, *Journey in Time*, pp. 212–213.

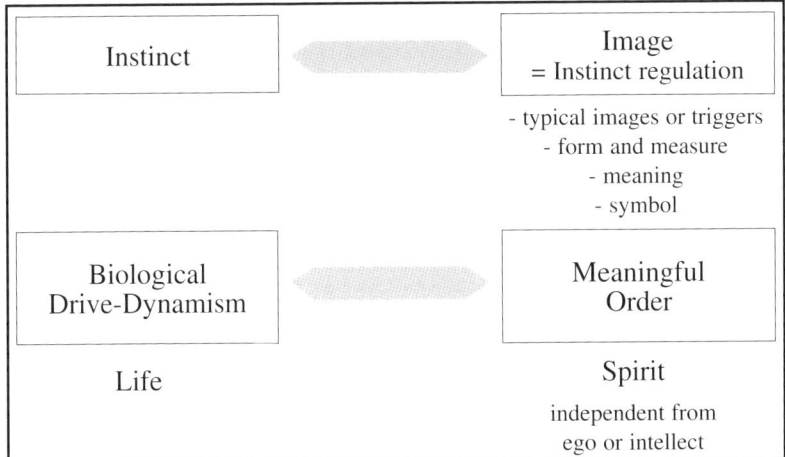

Fig. 10: The self-regulating (compensatory) relationship between instinct and image.

compensatory relationship—a system of "checks and balances". This interaction is summarized here in figure 10.

C.G. Jung reflects further on this connection between instinct and instinct regulation in his late work «*Mysterium Coniunctionis*». His statements reveal the *religious dimension* of pictures from the inner world: «The primary connection between image and instinct explains the interdependence of instinct and religion in the most general sense. These two spheres are in a mutually compensatory relationship, and by 'instinct' we must understand not merely 'eros' but everything that goes by the name of 'instinct'. 'Religion' on the primitive level means the psychic regulatory system that is coordinated [in a compensatory manner—author's note] with the dynamism of instinct. On a higher level, this primary interdependence is sometimes lost, and then religion can easily become an antidote to instinct, whereupon the originally compensatory relationship degenerates into conflict, religion petrifies into formalism, and instinct is vitiated. A split of this kind is not due to mere accident, nor is it a meaningless catastrophe. It lies rather in the nature of the evolutionary process itself, in the increasing extension and differentiation of consciousness. For just as there is no energy without the tension of opposites, so there can be no consciousness without the perception of differences. But any stronger emphasis of differences leads to polarity and finally to a conflict which maintains the necessary tension of opposites. This tension is needed on the one hand for increased energy production and on the other for the further differentiation of differences, both of which are indispensable requisites for the development of consciousness.»[18]

---

[18] C.G. Jung, *Mysterium Coniunctionis* [Coll. Works 14], § 603.

Wherever humans suspend the flow of a non-understandable or meaningless drive (aggression, sexual drivenness, compulsion, craving etc.), this is an act of reflection. Jung regarded this possibility for humans to reflect also as a drive of humans: that drive which makes us human. He writes: «There is another instinct, different from the drive to activity and so far as we know specifically human, which might be called the reflective instinct. Ordinarily we do not think of 'reflection' as ever having been instinctive, but associate it with a conscious state of mind. *Reflexio* means 'bending back' and, used psychologically, would denote the fact that the reflex, which carries the stimulus over into an instinctive discharge is interfered with by psychization. Owing to this interference, the psychic processes exert an attraction on the impulse to act excited by the stimulus. Therefore, before having discharged itself into the external world, the impulse is deflected into an endopsychic activity. *Reflexio* is a turning inwards, with the result that, instead of an instinctive action, there ensues a succession of derivative contents or states which may be termed reflection or deliberation, thus in place of the compulsive act there appears a certain degree of freedom, and in place of predictability a relative unpredictability as to the effect of the impulse.»[19] A little later Jung clarifies the transformation of an instinctual stimulus into a picture: «The richness of the human psyche and its essential character are probably determined by this reflective instinct. Reflection re-enacts the process of excitation and carries the stimulus over into a series of images which, if the impetus is strong enough, are reproduced in some form of expression. This may take place directly, for instance in speech; or may appear in the form of abstract thought, dramatic representation, or ethical conduct; or again, in a scientific achievement or a work of art».[20] Something that was a natural drive becomes something conscious, for example the bear-drive is depicted as bearman or the bird-drive as birdman. Jung regarded this reflection and hence the transformation of a drive stimulus into a conscious psychic content (that is into an image as we have seen) as «the cultural instinct *par excellence*, and its strength is shown in the power of culture to maintain itself in the face of untamed nature».[21] We shall now see that this drive regulation in humans has universal patterns.

---

[19] C.G. Jung, *Structure and Dynamics of the Psyche* [Coll. Works 8], § 241.
[20] C.G. Jung, op. cit., § 242.
[21] C.G. Jung, op. cit., § 243.

1.4. Universal Patterns of Imagination

As previously mentioned, instincts of animals are activated and restricted by images which trigger off something from within. Correlated with the different instincts we also find common patterns of feelings, ideas, symbolic images, judgements etc. in human beings.

Here is an example: hunter and gatherer societies relate to the spiritual side of life through tribal members who have a special ability to communicate with the spiritual powers of the other world. They are called medicine men or shamans. In 1945, a researcher in this field, A.P. Elkin, wrote about his fieldwork across the Australian continent: «At first sight, there is nothing stranger in anthropological literature and in fieldwork than the descriptions given by Aboriginal medicine men of the way in which they received their power. .... But [...] the striking fact is not so much the weirdness of the details as their similarity over wide regions of the continent, and even in apparently widely separated regions. In other words, we are confronted by a prescribed pattern of ritual experience through which medicine men are made.»[22] Other ethnologists also described such «prescribed patterns of ritual experience» referring to similar rituals outside Australia and in fact all over the world. We meet a universal phenomenon, which is not explainable by migration. That such patterns are somehow part of human nature is made evident by comparative research into religion, mythology and social behaviour, revealing that their basic structures share many similar features.[23] We find such similarities among cultures that were certainly not in contact with each other. Examples from all over the world show that humans are to some extent «pre-programmed» by their instincts but have acquired a certain amount of free will (see Fig. 11).[24]

In addition to these outer situations and mythological ideas, C.G. Jung also observed that in dreams of modern humans, one quite frequently finds motifs and sequences containing mythological elements that are completely unknown to the dreamer. In children's dreams in particular, he

---

[22] A.P. Elkin, *Aboriginal Men of High Degree: Initiation and Sorcery in the World's Oldest Tradition*, p. 18.
[23] See, for example, the work of M. Eliade and I. Eibl-Eibesfeldt.
[24] See I. Eibl-Eibesfeldt, *Human Ethology*, pp. 86–87.

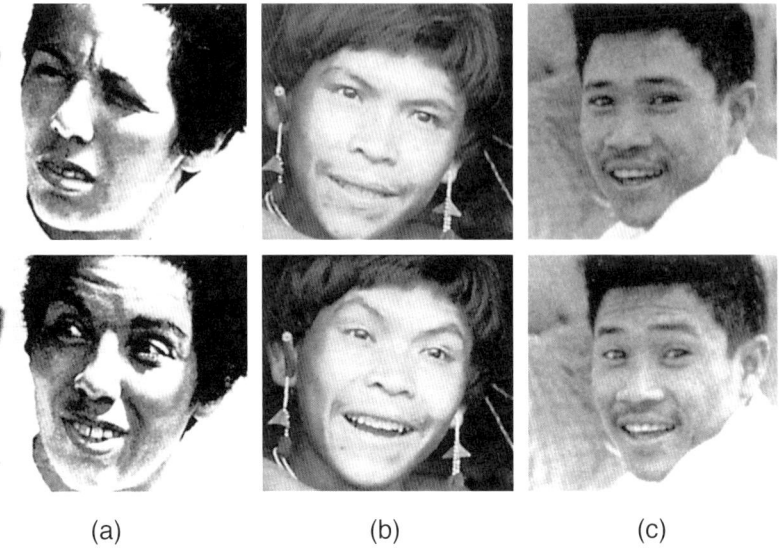

(a)   (b)   (c)

Fig. 11: Examples of «eye-brow flash», a rapid eyebrow movement as an expression of readiness to make social contact, seen in every culture. This was observed by the human ethologist I. Eibl-Eibesfeldt, who could make evident that humans are to a certain degree «pre-programmed» by their instincts. The pictures above (a) show a French woman, above (b) a Yanomami man, and above (c) a Balinese man. [27]

found impressive evidence that something inside—a spiritual factor unknown to the dreamer—knows something more than the person who has the dream.[25] This is nothing new to hunter and gatherer societies. It is well documented for example that the traditional Naskapi people even speak about an inner, greater human that knows more than we do, and who speaks to us in dreams.[26]

All these observations led the psychiatrist C.G. Jung to the hypothesis that there must be organizing factors in the human psyche which form and structure human ideas and feelings. In accordance with Western traditions, he called these basic spiritual structures *archetypes*. He called, as already mentioned, the centring archetype that seems to be the basis of the development of ego-consciousness, the Self. Usually humans are not conscious of these archetypes. They are the inherited basic structure of the collective unconscious of human beings.

---

[25]   C.G. Jung, *Seminare Kinderträume* (on Children's Dream Seminars), p. 28.
[26]   F.G. Speck, *Naskapi—The Savage Hunters of the Labrador Peninsula*, p. 35.
[27]   I. Eibl-Eibesfeldt, *Human Ethology*, p. 457.

1.5. Archetype and Symbol

Archetypes are common organizing factors in the unconscious psyche, visible only through their effects in the form of archetypal pictures or symbols. Symbols are always the combined product of the archetype and the environment at a given moment. Accordingly, symbols are not inherited, since they are temporally, locally and individually determined. What is inherited are only their unconscious organizers, the *archetypes per se*. Therefore, as C.G. Jung emphazised again and again, we must make a careful distinction between the *archetype as such* and the *archetypal image or symbol*. The latter is the result of the ordering effect of the former. A comparison with the growth of a crystal may illustrate this difference (Fig. 12).

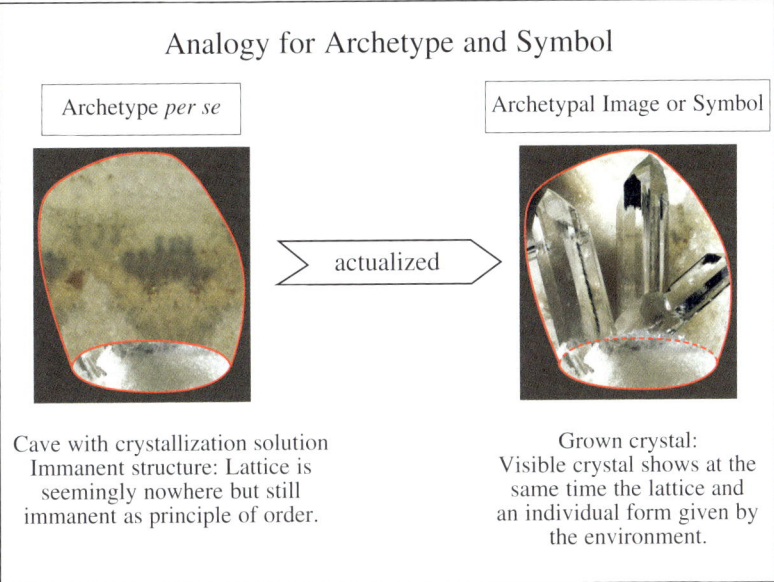

Fig. 12: A symbol, which comes out of an archetype, could be compared with a crystal, which grows out of a liquid.

A crystal is born out of a densely saturated solution and grows according to general physical-chemical laws. A salt-crystal grows out of a salty solution, a candy-crystal grows out of a sugar-solution, each having its own typical geometric structure. But the final shape of the crystal will be individual, determined by local conditions.

An archetype would correspond to the basic structure of the potential crystal, a structure that cannot be seen as long as the crystal is not born. But as soon as there is a crystal, we can deduce that in the mother-solution this specific ordering factor was present. In a comparable manner, archetypes of the collective unconscious are usually invisible. But when they become actualized by inner or outer forces, they start their organizing activity, which they exert on human ideas, emotions and images. It is only by this organizing activity that they become visible. Thus, the mani-festation of the archetype is the archetypal image or symbol. From the symbols we can see what archetype is mainly activated.

In the same way, painting a picture mirrors the actual pattern in the psychic background. Painting includes a lot of coincidences of different choices which reflect this pattern, e.g. the choice of paper and material for painting, the chosen colours, the chosen format (size, horizontal or vertical). Thus we can say that pictures mirror the situation of the soul. Based on this, various tests have been developed, e.g. colour symbolism tests, space symbolism tests, tests like the coin-test, or motive symbolism tests like the tree-, family-, or the village-test. Graphology is also based on this knowledge, making use of elements such as organisation, proportion and movement.

Each of these tests brings one or several aspects of picture interpretation into the foreground. In the Jungian perspective of understanding pictures we will consider the symbolism of all aspects by amplifying every element. We ask the picture to reveal its meaning: we do not force upon it a theory of meaning. We try to follow the still unknown tendency of the symbolic nature of the picture that we can express only by analogies. Jung emphazises this by stating: «If symbols mean anything at all, they are tendencies which pursue a definite but not yet recognizable goal and consequently can express themselves only in analogies. In this uncertain situation one must be content to leave things as they are, and give up trying to know anything beyond the symbol.» Later he adds: «... symbols are tendencies whose goal is as yet unknown. .... long before they [the unconscious tendencies] reach consciousness, certain unconscious tendencies betray their presence by symbols, occurring mostly in dreams but also in waking fantasies and symbolic actions».[28] Thus in order for the symbolic expression of the unconscious to be able to enter and unfold on the conscious level one has to respect the symbols and let them come alive.

---

[28] C.G Jung, *Mysterium Coniunctionis* [Coll. Works 14], § 668.

1.6. Images as Bridges to the Unconscious

The painting of a mood, a problem or spontaneously appearing fantasies or dreams—all express something of the unconscious background which contains a wealth of consciously unknown emotion and knowledge. This is the reason why these images allow us to contact our inner background. Especially in cases when there are no dreams, painting may be a way to establish contact with the unconscious. Jung said about his own exerience with pictures: «At any time of my life when I came up against a blank wall, I painted a picture or hewed stone. Each such experience proved to be *a rite d'entrée* for the ideas and works that followed hard upon it».[29]

Trying to create these inner images can often be the *first step* towards connecting to the inner world. This is generally acknowledged as helpful and healing, and is widely used today in psychiatric clinics and art therapy. By painting pictures of the inner world, one becomes receptive to an inspiration from the unconscious, opening up another and unknown world. The description of the personal experience of Jung in his encounter with the unconscious is quite helpful in understanding the value of images. He writes: «To the extent that I managed *to translate the emotions into images*—that is to say, to find the images which were concealed in the emotions—I was inwardly calmed and reassured. Had I left those images hidden in the emotions, I might have been torn to pieces by them. There is a chance that I might have succeeded in splitting them off; but in that case I would inexorably have fallen into a neurosis and so been ultimately destroyed by them anyhow. As a result of my experiment I learned how helpful it can be, from the therapeutic point of view, to find the particular images which lie behind emotions.»[30]

Then follows a *second step*, namely *the understanding of the meaning* that is expressed in these pictures. People in general and especially artists sometimes paint the most amazing symbolic pictures. But then they often do not find the necessary time to ponder over their creations and consequently do not work on the meaning of what they have produced.

---

[29] C.G. Jung, *Memories, Dreams, Reflections*, p. 175.
[30] C.G. Jung, op. cit, p. 177.

Usually such reflections lead to further images that develop in a certain meaningful way. More than once in this process of creating a picture series I was able to observe how my paintbrush started to move out on its own, so to speak. I just had to allow what wanted to come out of the unconscious to emerge.

In the beginning of the analytical work, this understanding of the picture's meaning is the task of the analyst. It is important, however, that these insights only flow *indirectly* into the analytical work in order not to disturb the spontaneous flow of pictures. Speaking about the role of the analyst, Jung says: «I felt bound to insist that they [the pictures as manifestation of the unconscious] were baffling, if only to stop myself from framing, on the basis of certain theoretical assumptions, interpretations, which I felt were not only inadequate but liable to prejudice the ingenuous productions of the patient. .... I always took good care to let the interpretation of each image tail off into a question whose answer was left to the free fantasy-activity of the patient.»[31]

In this way, pictures become a bridge to the unknown spirit of the psychic background. While working with the unconscious, especially when patients remember few dreams or none at all, this is a way of gaining access to the unconscious spirit. The method of picture interpretation can help towards understanding this unique spiritual creative force behind moods, cravings, desires, compulsions etc.

It is crucial not only to turn patiently towards the forming of pictorial expressions of the soul, but also to learn to understand them by patient attention in order to distill their meaning. One not only needs to paint and understand the painting but might have to repaint it and understand it anew. This is what Jung did with his dreams and visions as the so-called «Red Book» shows (Fig. 13)—he never became tired of trying to express his inner images and repainting the most important ones. «*In patientia vestra habetis animas vestras.*» («You will obtain your souls by your patience.») This alchemical sentence was so important for Jung that he painted it on the wall of his tower in Bollingen.

Fig. 13: A page from the so-called «Red Book» of C.G. Jung, where he painted the images of his own night-journey. This experience of diving into his own unconscious was the trigger for further research that consolidated Jung's hypothesis of a common or collective unconscious.

---

[31] C.G. Jung, *Structure and Dynamics of the Psyche* [Coll. Works 8], § 400.

çatapatha-brâhmaṇam 2, 2, 4.

Thus, according to Jung, intensive brooding over the meaning of symbols of the unconscious makes them come *alive*.

In this book, we will try to find access to a better understanding of the pictorial expressions of the unconscious. We mainly do this in order to better understand our own pictures, which come from the depths of the psyche. And the better we are able to understand ourselves, the better we can understand the pictures of other people in the process of analytical work. We can again round off this second step with an account by Jung of his own relationship with his *anima*. (This term he used for that part of a man's psyche, which is the personified inner bridge to the unconscious world of images.) He writes: «But the anima ... communicates the images of the unconscious to the conscious mind, and that is what I chiefly valued her for. For decades I always turned to the anima when I felt that my emotional behaviour was disturbed, and that something had been constellated in the unconscious. I would then ask the anima: «Now what are you up to? *What do you see?* I should like to know.» After some resistance *she regularly produced an image.* As soon as the image was there, the unrest or the sense of oppression vanished. The whole energy of these emotions was transformed into interest in and curiosity about the image. *I would speak with the anima about the images* she communicated to me, *for I had to try to understand them as best I could, just like a dream.*»[32]

Then comes, the crucial *third step* that Jung calls «drawing the ethical conclusions from them [the images]».[33] After the meaning of these inner images has been freed and become conscious, this acquired insight from the depths of the unconscious has to be *reunited with the individual reality*. Jung writes about this phase of his own work: «I took great care to try to understand every single image, every item of my psychic inventory, and to classify them scientifically—so far as this was possible—and, above all, to realize them in actual life. That is what we usually neglect to do. We allow the images to rise up, and maybe we wonder about them, but that is all. We do not take the trouble to understand them, let alone draw ethical conclusions from them. This stopping-short conjures up the negative effects of the unconscious.»[34] The pictures which C.G. Jung created in his «Red Book», chiselled in stone or painted in his tower in Bollingen, finally found their way into words in his scientific work. There he tried to bring into his life the insights he obtained from pondering on the meaning of these images.

---

[32] C.G. Jung, *Memories, Dreams, Reflections,* pp. 187–188; (my italics).
[33] C.G. Jung, op. cit, p. 192.
[34] Ibid.

1.7. Effects of Pictures

«If you paint the devil on the wall, he will come» is a popular German saying. A picture can have a magical effect and constellate that which has been imagined in the realm of consciousness. This is a warning not to have a naïve or light-hearted attitude towards imagination, towards creating images, because they can, as we have seen, trigger off an instinct that can lead to something positive or negative, depending on the attitude of the painter.

This magical effect of creating pictures is a first step in transforming an emotion. In particular, any autonomous content that is represented by a picture reaches consciousness in this way. Thus *Auseinandersetzung* (≈ inner debate) becomes possible. In therapy, therefore, it is often advisable to connect to overwhelming fantasies by painting whatever is irritating (see Fig. 15–17). The same is true for dreams and visions. Painting is also often recommended when there is a danger of dissociation as it forces different elements into one frame. Another benefit is that pictures contain and unite opposites, because they are created out of a collaboration of consciousness with the unconscious, that has a transformative effect on both of them (see Fig. 14). But in spite of this indisputable beneficial and healing effect, resistance to painting must be respected.

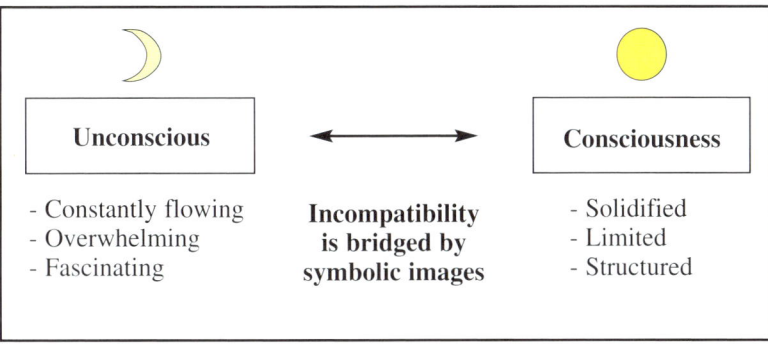

Fig. 14: The incompatibility of the conscious and the unconscious world is bridged by images, which are recognized as symbols.

Fig. 15: Picture painted in finger-paint by a 24-year-old woman with a mouse phobia. In the beginning she could only paint the tail of the mouse. She had to stop as she was horrified by what she saw.

Fig. 16: The fact that she could later finish the first painting encouraged her to continue to care and to paint the horrifying «other».

Fig. 17: The surprising redeeming effect came when the horrifying «other» received a name: Ferdinand. It was the beginning of a *humanizing* of this daemonic autonomous complex.

Often, the symbols mediating between the unconscious (moon-world) and consciousness (sun-world) appear in a strange, non-rational, overwhelming and sometimes frightening form. We can easily call them daemonic or divine. With regard to this, Jung writes: «It is not a matter of indifference whether one calls something a 'mania' or a 'god'. To serve a mania is detestable and undignified, but to serve a god is full of meaning and promise because it is an act of submission to a higher, invisible, and spiritual being. The personification enables us to see the relative reality of the autonomous system, and not only makes its assimilation possible but also depotentiates the daemonic forces of life. When the god is not acknowledged, egomania develops, and out of this mania comes sickness.»[35]

This depotentiating effect we find, for instance, in the myth of Perseus. Mirroring—reflecting—the horrible face of the Gorgon made it possible for Perseus to cut off her head and out of her came Pegasus, the winged horse. Later on Perseus killed the sea-dragon Cetos, thus redeeming Andromeda, the daughter of Kepheus and Cassiopeia, king and queen of Ethiopia. All these figures became immortal in the starry sky in winter; we can see them as archetypal star-constellations.

To experience the magical effect of pictures we must pay attention to how to relate to pictures painted by patients. Jung points out this problem explicitly: «The pictures should be given back to the patient because they are very important. You can get copies; patients like to do copies for the doctor. But he should leave the originals with the patients, because they want to look at them; and when they look at them they feel that their unconscious is expressed. The objective form works back on them and they become enchanted. The suggestive influence of the picture reacts on the psychological system of the patient and induces the same effect, which he put into the picture. That is the reason for idols, for the magic use of sacred images, of icons. They cast their magic into our system and put us right, provided we put ourselves into them. Take a Lamaic mandala, which has a Buddha in the centre, or a Shiva, and, to the extent that you can put yourself into it, it answers and comes into you. It has a magic effect.»[36]

Let us illustrate the effect of understanding an overwhelming impulse by looking at two alchemical pictures from the 16th century (see Fig. 18 and 19). In such a process we let an emerging, bewildering or overwhelming emotion or affect enter the «vessel» of the picture. (In alchemic language «we let the dragon enter the vessel and close it hermetically».) That means we do not identify with it. Then we look at what happens with this picture, how it transforms, for example, by holding the

---

[35] C.G. Jung, *Alchemical Studies* [Coll. Works 13], § 55.
[36] C.G. Jung, *The Symbolic Life* [Coll. Works 18], § 413.

tension of the suspended drivenness, aggression, craving etc. (In alchemy this is called the *opus contra naturam*, the «work against nature».) This leads to a freeing of the image behind the emotion and to the birth of a uniting symbol.

Fig. 18: The mystery of physical attraction of bodies or matter was the main concern of alchemy. To accept the existence of such «unorthodox energies» and to look at them was the prerequisite of the work, the *prima materia* as they called it. What we see here is a picture from a 16th-century manuscript, showing the physical attraction of man and woman—outside in a landscape.[37] It is an initial attempt to contain this energy in a frame.

---

[37] C. Hartung, *Das "Kunstbüchlein" des Alchemisten Caspar Hartung vom Hoff*, fol. 35r.

Effects of Pictures 37

Fig. 19: The main objective of alchemical work was to put the «mystery of physical attraction of matter» in a vessel and to look at it, ponder over it and see what comes out of it. This process was called "distillation" in alchemy. Below are a man and woman united inside the vessel; while above them, as vapours at the top of the vessel, the sun and moon are also uniting in love. This makes the archetypal or divine dimension—which is behind any overwhelming attraction—recognizable. This has a redeeming effect on the ego-consciousness as the transpersonal dimension of the psyche becomes visible and thus the *meaning* of any drivenness or craving is extracted.[38]

We need to look at the picture which emerges as a result of being contained «in the retort», to ponder over it and try to extract its meaning. The next part of the book, Part 2, is a proposal as to how we could proceed to understand pictures in this respect.

---

[38] C. Hartung, *Das "Kunstbüchlein" des Alchemisten Caspar Hartung vom Hoff*, fol. 36v.

Part 2

Proposal for a Method in Picture Interpretation

In Chymicis verfanti Natura, Ratio, Experientia & lectio, fint Dux, fcipio, perfpicilia & lampas.

Fig. 20: Guiding image for the work of the alchemist. The text to this picture *«Dux tibi natura»* (May Nature be Your Guide) points to the central issue in the *«artis auriferae»*, the «art of creating gold», i.e. consciousness. (From Michael Maier *Atalanta fugiens*, Frankfurt 1618, emblem 42.) The Latin text above the image means: «For those who want to get involved in the work of alchemy, let nature, reason, experience and reading be their guide, their staff, their spectacles and their lamp» [author's translation].

2.1. Interpretation as the «Art of Creating Consciousness»

The aim of Part 2 is to find a way to develop our ability to «read pictures». A useful form of training is to read a picture without being given any personal context, other than the age and gender of the author. In this way, we are obliged to look for a way to make the picture reveal its hidden meaning out of itself, something that can be assumed to be possible for any image coming from the inner unconscious world.

To enable a picture to start to talk to us «out of itself», we have to *ask the picture questions*. Through this dialogue each interpretation becomes an act of creating consciousness out of a picture. It is an extracting of its immanent meaning through our interpretation. This meaning has to be translated into words by our conscious mind, which is, of course, not a neutral camera lens but an individually shaped entity. For this reason we have to be aware of the fact that our individual disposition, with its complexes, interferes with the interpretation of anything unknown.

Fortunately, human consciousness is not just infinitely individual but shows typical general features as well. We speak of a *typology* of humans. From earliest times, attempts have been made to classify individuals according to types, and so bring order into the chaos. The oldest attempts known to us were made by oriental astrologers, and in ancient Greece with the division into four temperaments by humours.[1] Human typology has been the subject of human interest ever since.

C.G. Jung proposed a new typology, based on the two main attitudes of humans—which he called extravert and introvert—as well as on the four functions of consciousness: sensation, feeling, thinking and intuition. This typology has proved helpful in the art of creating consciousness. As our typology also has a strong influence on the way we look at things, we now need to pay special attention to our mental set-up.

---

[1] See C.G. Jung, *Psychological Types* [Coll. Works 8], § 933 and M.-L. von Franz, *C.G. Jung, His Myth in Our Time*, p. 47 n32.

a. The Two Attitudes

C.G. Jung first distinguished between the extravert and the introvert attitude. In the case of an extravert it is the outer object which most interests the subject, while with the introvert the attention will first flow from the object back to the subject. This is to say that the introvert will first become aware of his own inner reaction to a specific object before he can fully concentrate on the object itself. Jung compared this movement and countermovement of psychic energy with Goethe's concept of *systole* and *diastole*, stating that both attitudes are present in everyone; the type is determined merely by the fact that the one or the other attitude customarily predominates. The attitude can change with the passage of time. The introvert, generally speaking, is characterized by a reflective nature, which causes them always to think and consider before acting. This naturally makes persons of this type slow to act. Their shyness and distrust of things induces hesitation, and so they always have difficulty in adapting to the external world. The extraverts, on the other hand, have an open, forthcoming disposition, which is at home in every situation. Their outgoing nature makes it difficult to notice and adapt to the needs of the inner world. Jung's differentiation of extraverted and introverted types has been so widely recognized that the two concepts have entered the vocabulary of ordinary speech.[2]

Respect for the Introverted Attitude

In picture analysis, we naturally concentrate mostly on an outer (exterior) object. This gives rise to the danger that we do not pay sufficient attention to our introverted attitude, which is characterized by one's attention flowing from the object back to the subject. In order to avoid this danger, we must make a special effort *to pay close attention to our very first subjective reaction to a picture.* Ask: «What is my «gut-reaction»? This kind of response must not be lost.

Then as a second step, it has proved helpful to note our inner reactions to the picture as completely as possible. For this it makes sense to be aware of our four functions—details of which will follow on the next pages.

With the *sensation* function we might ask: «How does my body react to this picture?»

With the *feeling* function we might ask: «Do I like/dislike this picture?» Or: «Does it drain/boost my energy?»

With the *thinking* function we might ask: «Does the picture leave me with an ordered, peaceful mind?» Or: «Are things congruent?»

---

[2] See C.G. Jung, *Psychological Types* [Coll. Works 6], §§ 556ff. and M.-L. von Franz, *C.G. Jung, His Myth in Our Time*, p. 46.

Interpretation as the «Art of Creating Consciousness»

With the *intuitive* function we might ask, especially if I am the analyst of the author of a picture: «Could I work analytically with that person?» Or: «Does the picture 'smell' healthy?» Or: «Is the picture hinting at something to worry about?»

The first impression of a picture is based on such an initial circumambulation with the four functions. I invite you to do this with this picture by a 28-year-old woman (see Fig. 21). She had the following dream, which she brought to me, together with this picture.

Fig. 21: Dream and picture of a 28-year-old woman. The French text of the dream reads: «A woman and a man, wearing medieval clothes, carry a big white egg. They intend to put it between two objects, resembling loudspeakers, which will ventilate it in order that it [the egg] can be aired». Try to ask the suggested questions regarding your inner reactions.

THE EXTRAVERTED ATTITUDE

After this first step of looking inside to our subjective reaction, we now turn to the object itself, the picture. Of course, we must try as far as possible to avoid mixing up our own subjective ideas with the objective message of the picture. For this, certain criteria and proven scales are needed. These will be dealt with in Part 3 of this book.

But before we deal with criteria and scales, we shall concentrate on a working procedure within which these criteria can be usefully applied. The procedure is based on the four functions of consciousness, and so we shall turn to them first.

b. The Four Functions of Consciousness

Marie-Louise von Franz pointed out that «the conscious ego in the human being is an unfathomable mystery, no matter how familiar and subjective it may seem to us. ... It is the centre and subject of all conscious personal acts and all willed efforts and achievements in adaptation».[3] When Jung studied the way in which individuals adapt to their environment with their ego, he discovered that one could divide these attempts of adaptation into the following four basic forms of psychic activity or of psychological functions.[4]

1. The *sensation function* registers consciously the facts that we find in the picture. We could ask: «What is the quality of the paper, the medium, the frame, the format, the colours etc.? Which elements do we see?»

2. The *feeling function* establishes the value order within the picture. We could ask: «What was important/unimportant/central to the author? Where is his/her energy?»

3. The *thinking function* looks at the structure and logical order among the different elements of the picture. We could ask: «What is the proportion of elements to each other? How are they organized? Are they moving? How is the space symbolism connected to the colours etc.?»

4. The *intuitive function* appears to be a kind of perception via the unconscious, giving us hunches about the author of the picture. We could ask: «From what sort of constellation in the unconscious does this picture originate?» Or: «In which direction will this person probably develop?»

The four functions provide us with a complete basic orientation when trying to bring the immanent meaning of a picture to consciousness. So we can look at a picture in four different ways corresponding to our four functions.

Usually in the course of time every human develops one dominant function that is then also mainly used when approaching something new.

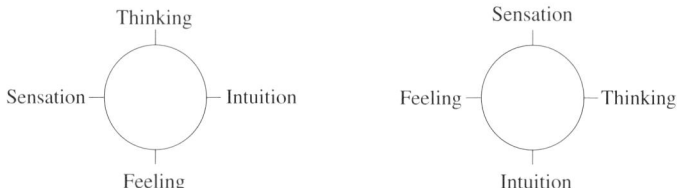

Fig. 22: The four functions of ego-consciousness according to C.G. Jung.

---

3   M.-L. von Franz, *C.G. Jung, His Myth in Our Time*, p. 45f.
4   Ibid. p. 46.

This *main function* (in figures 22 and 23 represented on the top of the circle) becomes in this way quite reliable and differentiated. It may tend to dominate the way one looks at a picture.

On the other hand, the function that is standing opposite to the main function usually remains undifferentiated. This does not mean that it does not exist. But one could say that it is rather «stubborn», being not always easily available to the ego. Jung calls it the *inferior function*. For instance, a sensation type will find it difficult to activate his intuition or a thinking type will have to make an effort to activate his feeling function.

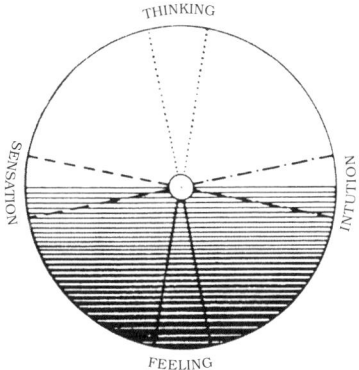

Fig. 23: Diagram showing the four functions of consciousness. Thinking, the superior function in this case, which is mostly near consciousness, at the centre of attention, occupies the centre of the *light* half of the circle; whereas feeling, the inferior function, which is mostly far-off consciousness and receives only minor attention, occupies the bottom of the *dark* half. The two auxiliary functions are partly in the light and partly in the dark.[5]

In order to prevent a one-sided approach to a picture, it is helpful to be aware of our main function as well as our weak spot, our inferior function, and in the course of picture interpretation to systematically give energy to each function.

---

[5] C.G. Jung, *Psychology and Alchemy* [Coll. Works 12], § 137, Fig. 49.

2.2. A Possible Way to Proceed

a. Circumambulation with the Four Functions

In order to visualize this extraverted circumambulation, we apply an old alchemical pattern, putting the four elements (earth, water, air and fire) into a circular order and attributing the four functions of consciousness to them (see Fig. 24).[6] Moving from element to element, from function to function, we start with *sensation*; that is, with describing the solid facts, such as the painting material, paper format, formal aspects, colours chosen, different elements. This would correspond to the earth. Step by step we move now from the hard dry facts, as it were, to the more subtle insights.

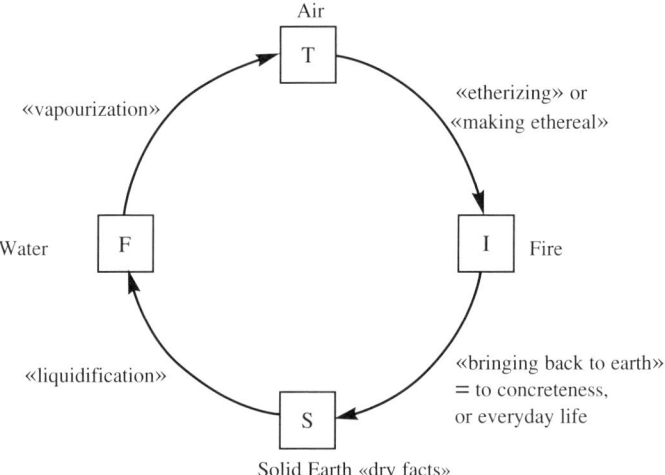

Fig. 24: First circumambulation: We start to describe the picture with the four functions: Sensation (S), Feeling (F), Thinking (T) and Intuition (I). There is an increase in subtleness from earth to water to air to fire.

---

[6] This method was inspired by the alchemical statement of Maria the Hebrew (probably living in Egypt in the 1st to 3rd century): «Turn the earth into water and the water into air and the air into fire, then you would reach the wisdom». (See Th. Abt, *The Great Vision of Moḥammad Ibn Umail*, p. 24).

Next we come to the *feeling function*, where things start to flow: we see what value is given to the different elements in the picture, i.e. what is more important to the author of the picture and what is less so. Then we move on to the still more subtle «airy» *thinking function,* connecting the different elements, considering for example what colour is in what area of the picture and how it is related to other elements. As the last and «subtlest function», *intuition* tells us where this image is coming from and to what possible development it might be pointing. With this last function, which is as subtle as fire so to speak, a spark might be kindled indicating what the whole circumambulation with the four functions is going to result in—that is, a first assumption or hypothesis.

b. The Hypothesis and its Opposite

By the circumambulation of a picture with our four functions we arrive at a hypothesis or assumption about what might be constellated in the unconscious of the author when painting that image. This quintessence

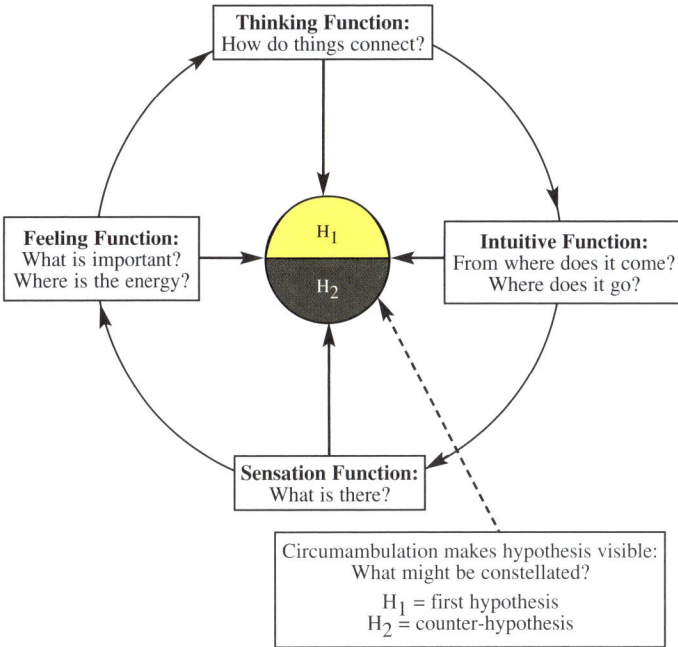

Fig. 25: The circumambulation of the picture using the four functions of consciousness, resulting in the fifth, the quintessence, so to speak: the formulation of a hypothesis and its opposite, the counter-hypothesis.

of our work with the four functions cannot—and this must be emphasised—take place without the help of the unconscious. We speak in German of an *Einfall*, meaning that a thought or insight came from outside, literally «falling into the mind». We never can produce an *Einfall*, but we can create the necessary attitude that can invite an *Einfall* to come; and then we need to be receptive, to receive what «falls in» and to hold on to it.

The formulation of a hypothesis is very helpful as it *activates our interest* in finding out whether this assumption is confirmed by the different elements of the picture or not.

However, any formulated hypothesis leads immediately to a subtle problem: as soon as I arrive at my hypothesis, I unconsciously start to 'love' it and thus might identify with «*my* discovered assumption». In so doing, I lose sight of other possibilities. For that reason we need to be our own devil's advocate and strive for the formulation of what I call a *counter-hypothesis* (see Fig. 25).

My key-experience for realizing the need for a counter-hypothesis took place in a session of my control-case colloquium at the C.G. Jung Institute in the early 1980s. A Japanese student presented a most beautifully painted picture from one of her patients in Japan, giving us, as usual, just his age and gender. The group, myself included, worked for around an hour and came to the conclusion that the author of the picture must be a gifted person with a certain inner ambivalence and hence a potential for development in analysis. This was based on a strongly felt energy that made us all feel optimistic and positive towards the picture and its author. At the end of our interpretation the Japanese student informed us—with a gentle smile—that the author of the picture had painted it in a clinic and had a diagnosed schizophrenia. During the whole time we were working on the picture, she was of course not supposed to say a word about her patient. Her features were inscrutable. As these case colloquia also serve as an experiment as to whether this method of interpretation pictures is any good, that experience taught me a hard but valuable lesson. I realized how easily we could fall in love with a hypothesis and how one thus loses the critical attitude towards assumptions one has made. After we were told that the author of the picture had a diagnosed schizophrenia, we immediately recognized this aspect in the picture. But the beauty of the Japanese style of painting and the intensity of the energy in the picture had carried us all away. We only saw the positive side of the painting and the potential of its author. That literally made us blind to the dangerous aspects that were also there in the picture. After that experience, I started to bring in the *safety valve* of a counter-hypothesis by always asking: «What is the opposite of my assumption?» This enables us to retrieve what becomes naturally unconscious by our hypothesis, namely a different possibility of understanding the meaning of a picture.

There is also another reason that makes it necessary to search for the counter-hypothesis. As our hypothesis can point either to the state of the author of the picture or to a *compensation* for the present state, we need to be careful with our hypothesis. We have to be aware that the picture could mean just the opposite. For this reason we are only really on the safe side if we look for the counter-hypothesis, which needs to be the *contrary of the hypothesis.*

A third reason for formulating a counter-hypothesis is the fact that we have a tendency to project something we are unconscious of onto the unknown material that we are looking at and trying to understand. This is especially the case with abstract pictures, which invite us to indulge in our own fantasies.

The important thing with formulating a counter-hypothesis is that it forces us to *keep a healthy doubt.* In this tension of the «yes» and «no» the picture is given a chance to express itself.

c. From the «Living Cell» to the Interpretation

After the formulation of our hypothesis and counter-hypothesis, we proceed to a second round in which we further circumambulate with the four functions. We ask the picture whether there is any support for the hypothesis or rather for the counter-hypothesis (see Fig. 26). Every amplification of a criterion supports either the hypothesis (H_1) or the counter-hypothesis (H_2) and thereby shows which side is given more support. During the process of interpretation, the hypothesis and/or the counter-hypothesis sometimes becomes more precise or modified.

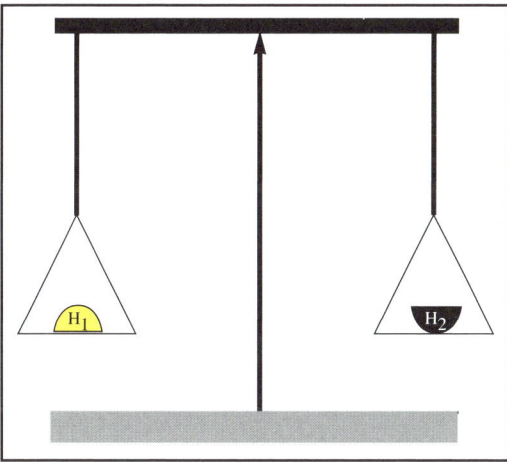

Fig. 26: The two hypotheses on the scales. Every amplification of a criterion supports either the hypothesis (H_1) or the counter-hypothesis (H_2) and thus shows which side is given more support.

In this way we can proceed in a more objective and hence more scientific way. Our counter-hypothesis is, in a way, a means of falsifying our hypothesis and thus *keeping alive our doubt that our hypothesis might be wrong*.

Each picture interpretation then becomes like the cultivation of something living: the hypothesis, together with the counter-hypothesis is like a *first living cell* that inspires further reflection. It has been born out of the four elements—our four functions. And out of this first cell our deeper interpretation grows by means of a second circumambulation. This will nourish the «first living cell» and allow the interpretation to grow organically.

At the end of this second circumambulation of the picture, our aim is to be able to give an answer to the following questions:

1. What is constellated: where does the picture come from?

Here we want to give a possible answer to the question of what constellation in the unconscious the picture originates from.

2. What is the relationship to the feminine principle?

By this we understand the relationship to reality, to mother nature, the body and of course to female individuals in general. Here we try to understand on what sort of soil the author of the picture is standing, what is her or his instinctual basis? What, symbolically speaking, is the relationship to earth and water?

3. What is the relationship to the masculine principle?

The answer to this question should give an idea about what spirit the author of the picture «lives in». What are the inherent values and spiritual orientation prevalent in the author? What is the relationship to the ordering principle, to meaning and to structures in life and of course to male individuals in general? What, symbolically speaking, is the relationship to air and fire?

4. In which direction might the development go?

What hints does the picture give us concerning negative or positive, destructive or constructive potentials?

5. What is the quintessence of the picture for our work?

What is the conclusion from the interpretation work, what is the consequence? As in dream interpretation, we have to be able to make a *summary* in one sentence, in order to be able to really connect the insight into the constellation of the unconscious pattern with consciousness. This would be the *quintessence* of our interpretation. Our intense examination of the picture gives birth to our interpretation, in some ways it is as if a baby is born. But whether or not this interpretation is really correct—whether «the baby» is truly alive—is not in our human hands alone, no method can guarantee it. Instead it is as if the meaning emerges out of the picture like the rising of the sun.

As an aid to our memory, the five key questions can be related to the symbolism of the four corners of a rectangular picture (see Fig. 27). For the theoretical background I refer to chapter 3.4 on space symbolism. But it must be emphasized that the following image is just an aid for remembering the five questions. It does not represent an identification of the four corners of the picture with these mentioned aspects!

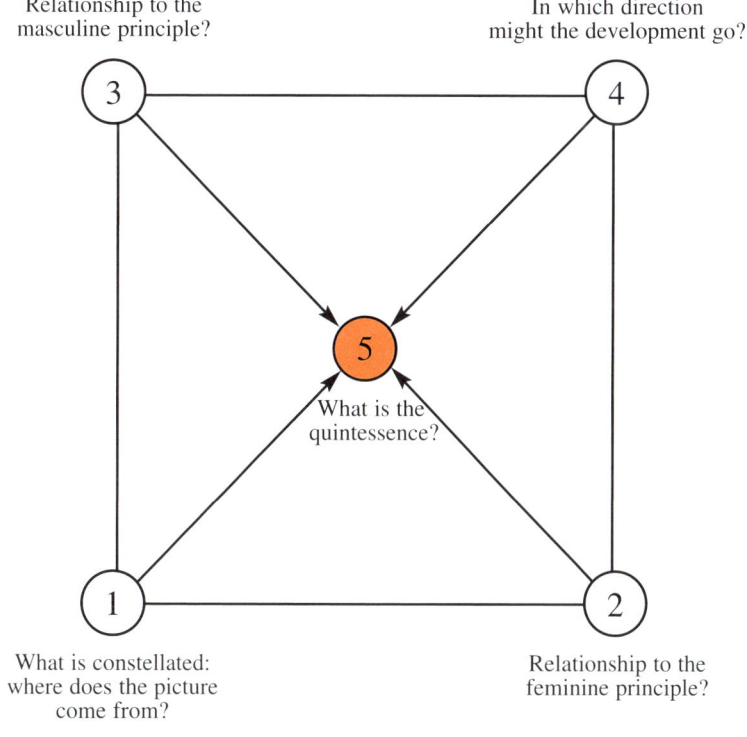

Fig. 27: Aide-mémoire for the five questions about the picture.

2.3. Dangers of Interpretation

Every interpretation, as an act of creating consciousness, consequently has a shadow. The most important danger is that of *interference* in the unfolding meaning of an individual. Jung writes on this: «I readily admit that I have such a great respect for what happens in the human soul that I would be afraid of disturbing and distorting the silent operation of nature by clumsy interference.»[7] And in another work he states: «I felt bound to insist that they [the pictures as manifestations of the unconscious] were baffling, if only to stop myself from framing, on the basis of certain theoretical assumptions, interpretations which I felt were not only inadequate but liable to prejudice the ingenuous productions of the patient. ... I always took good care to let the interpretation of each image tail off into a question whose answer was left to the free fantasy-activity of the patient.»[8]

This interference into the spontaneous expression of the soul is extremely tricky. I remember the period of my training at the Jung Institute in Zurich, when I started to work with people. A young student of psychology came to see me because of relationship problems and uncontrolled aggression. At one point he spontaneously brought me a portrait of himself, in which there were no ears (see Fig. 28). Looking at the picture, I asked him if he had problems with listening. He turned red and replied that his girlfriend had long been complaining that he did not listen to what others were saying. In the next session he again came with a portrait, this time with huge sausages on each side of the head, as ears (see Fig. 29). This

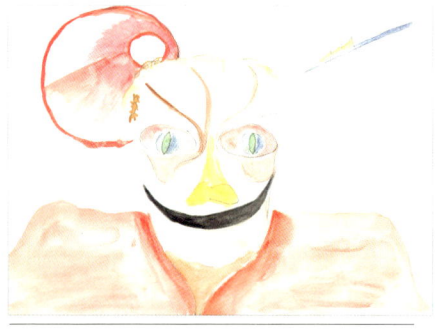

Fig. 28: Spontaneous portrait by a 24-year-old man.

---

[7] C.G. Jung, *Psychology and Alchemy* [Coll. Works 12], § 126.
[8] C.G. Jung, *Structure and Dynamics of the Psyche* [Coll. Works 8], § 400.

taught me not to link tricky questions directly to what can be seen on a picture, as this might inhibit the spontaneous flow of expression in images. In general there is *a danger of misusing the method of interpretation in a power-game, where one thinks one has to illuminate the other with the «wonderful insights» that we received from the picture.*

Fig. 29: Second portrait of the same man as for figure 28.

Another danger is the reducing of a picture or certain elements of it to: *«This is nothing but ... !»* I shall never forget a session with a male analyst at the beginning of my training. I painted a frog with a golden crown on its head. The analyst commented on the motif telling me that this, of course, was nothing genuine, but came from my knowing the fairy tale about the frog prince. Yet for me it was a spontaneous creation and I felt deeply hurt by this comment. The authority of the analyst left me speechless and did not allow me to reply to his reductive, cynical remark. I should have objected, telling him that I have to respect the image that comes into my mind, and not reduce the autonomy of the psyche to a *nothing but ...* .

After this general warning concerning picture interpretation in analytical sessions, we now have to give due attention to the dangers of interpreting a picture in detail. To this end, let us recall the specific pitfalls associated with every function:

The *sensation function* might make us get stuck in the details of dry, lifeless facts with no psychological statements or perspectives.

The *feeling function* might make us get stuck in vague, watery statements with no structure, order or so-called «red thread» in the interpretation.

The *thinking function* might make us get lost in a one-sided airy dry analysis and abstract constructions with no value order.

The *intuitive function* might make us get lost in wild speculations and ignore the simple facts. Instead of an interpretation, everything turns into a *«Rorschach Test»* that reveals a lot about the interpreter and little about the picture to be interpreted.

Whenever we become argumentative and emotional over what we are interpreting, we can be sure that we have lost our loving attitude towards the picture, because otherwise we would just turn to the picture and ask it whether our own point of view is correct.

2.4. Analysis and Synthesis

In the beginning, the picture is wholeness, complete in itself. This wholeness has to be opened up. People often do not like the idea that this unconscious wholeness must first be killed, cut into pieces, to enable us to look at its different parts. But then, later, the different pieces are seen together anew. And out of that, the same picture might become visible as a new unity. Out of the different elements of our interpretation there might in the end arise something alive, as if it were luminous, something with a *living meaning* that became conscious.

There is a way to proceed, a way from A to B (see Fig. 30): A would be the beginning when we first see the picture. It usually starts with our first reaction. Then follows the way of careful *analysis* of the picture. That means that we will have to familiarize ourselves with the different elements of the picture, one by one. At the end comes the *synthesis* of all the insights we obtained on the way, hopefully reaching B, our goal, the answer to the five questions (see page 50). We want to arrive at a picture interpretation that can be followed and also makes sense to a layperson. If all works well, the interpretation will become self-evident and convincing, leaving us at the end of our interpretation with new energy and life. With our respectful work, the life-giving *lumen naturae* or the *immanent meaning* of the picture will become visible, God willing.

We can now proceed along the proposed way, going from A to B. This is—of course—just one of several possible methods of interpreting pictures, but I have good reason to insist on this method instead of any other one. The word «method» originates from the Greek word *methodos* meaning way, but it is more than an ordinary way. It literally means «going after», «intensive search», «careful dealing» or «treatment of an object according to all rules of the art».[9] This is exactly what I would like to apply in picture interpretation. My reason for presenting this specific method of looking at pictures from the unconscious is that it *respects the picture in its own right*. The main means to achieve this goal is that we keep alive the *doubt* about the possible meaning of the picture. Every single aspect that we analyse can mean something or just its opposite. For instance, the numbers 11 or 13 are unlucky numbers because they encroach on the wholeness of the numbers 10 and 12, *but* their positive

---

[9] I thank Dr Ruedi Hoegger for pointing this meaning out to me.

Analysis and Synthesis 55

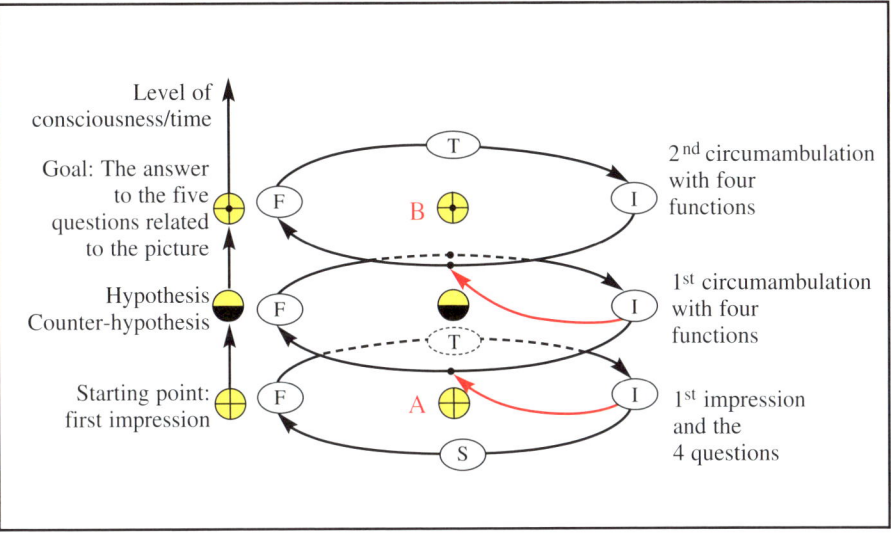

Fig. 30: This way from A to B has proved to be helpful in arriving safely at an interpretation that is respectful towards the picture, illuminating it with its own light. (Sensation (S), Feeling (F), Thinking (T) and Intuition (I)).

aspect is that they go beyond the 10 and the 12. For that reason, 11 and 13 can also symbolize a breaking up of a given completion that leads to new development and hence they can also be lucky numbers! Another example is the colour violet, which is not just a colour that points to a neurotic mixture of opposites, red and blue. It can definitely be that, but violet also symbolizes the union of opposites. All our criteria are in fact symbols that express an archetypal reality behind the symbol. And each archetype has the capability of both being constructive or destructive, depending on the attitude of the ego.[10] If we keep that in mind for every aspect that we analyse, we can maintain the necessary tension between the «yes» and the «no». Otherwise we would establish a fixed theory, and thus would *kill the living spirit* of the picture.

    The need for a method to come from A to B is paired with the need for a unique relationship that we have to establish with each and every picture that we ponder over. All methodological aids are merely tools that we apply to help us to see more clearly. And every tool is just as good as the person who applies it. But we know from tools in outer life that the right tool at the right time in the hands of the right person can be of great help. Tools are a help to the development of consciousness but they can, of course, also be misused. I am fully aware of that danger.

---

[10] See C.G. Jung, *Civilization in Transition* [Coll. Works 10], § 461.

When we speak of a root to a dentist, a gardener, or a mathematician they would probably all see something different. This makes us aware of a problem of perception: *we see what we are used to seeing, expect to see, and wish to see*. Our own experiences and expectations condition our views and thus how we interpret words and things around us. It is like that also with dreams and images: most times, we just cannot see the new, compensating, surprising message. To avoid this danger of prejudice and personal bias, we have to look for *objective criteria* for every element that we bring into focus. Jung called this procedure the collecting of associations and amplifications in order not only to familiarize ourself with the different elements of the picture but also to develop a point of view outside our conditioned view. This will now be looked at in detail in Part 3.

Part 3

Tools for Interpretation

AQVILA VOLANS PER AEREM ET BVFO gradiens per terram est Magisterium.

Fig. 31: «The eagle flying in the air and the toad creeping on earth contain the secret [*Magisterium*]», as the Latin text says. The opposites need to be always chained to each other. From *Symbola aurea mensa* by Michael Maier, p. 192.

3.1. Associations and Amplifications

Sigmund Freud used the method of *free associations* of his patients for dream interpretation. He let them start from the different motifs of the dream and by this method of association could enter into what he called the subconscious. C.G. Jung—who followed this approach of Freud's in the beginning—realized, however, that such free association could also start from anything in the world, as free associations lead necessarily to the unconscious complexes of the person.

When C.G. Jung attempted to understand his own dreams and those of people working with him, he saw that if he wanted to find out what dream symbols have to say on their own, he must remain focused on them. For that reason Jung started to apply a *disciplined association* for each motif and symbol (see Fig. 32). The personal associations to the different motifs and symbols, like personal memories, feelings etc., were one thing. Then non-personal associations also had to be collected as they give important hints for understanding the archetypal or transpersonal dimension of the dream. These non-personal associations he called amplifications.[1] In

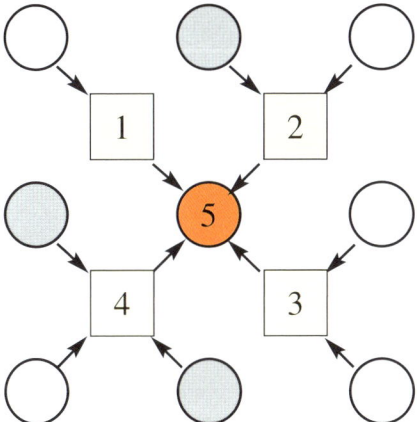

Fig. 32: The method of amplification of a dream according to C.G. Jung. A cluster of amplifications (○) and personal associations (○) clarifies the different symbols (1–4) of a dream and makes its central meaning (5) visible.

this way the vivifying meaning of the different dream symbols can be connected to consciousness.

We apply the same method to the different elements of a picture, assuming that it points to something unknown, like a dream. In order that this unknown meaning can become understandable, we collect all relevant associations and amplifications around each motif. The different elements of the picture, which get clarified in this way, finally point to the image's one meaning.

When we are given a picture during an analytical hour, it is helpful to let the author tell us the *personal associations,* answering questions like: What triggered the creation of the picture? Where was the starting point? What came to mind next? With that the picture remains in focus all the time, without being harmed by our prejudices or projections.

The work of *amplification,* which focuses on the archetypal level of the psyche—in the beginning of an analysis—is more the analyst's homework. It can be done alone or within the frame of a supervision hour or supervision group. When looking at a client's picture in a supervision group, an essential guideline is to maintain a respectful attitude towards both the picture and the client who created it—as if the client were present in the group. The «tools» for this amplification work are presented in the following chapters.

---

[1] See C.G. Jung, *Psychology and Alchemy* [Coll. Works 12], § 403. This method of collecting «necessary associations» in order to explain the inner meaning of symbols was rediscovered by C.G. Jung, who at that time could not have known that the old masters of Arabic alchemy already used this method hundreds of years before him. Muḥammad b. Aḥmad Abu al-Qāsim al-ʿIrāqī (12th century) even uses the word «necessary associations», that means the same as «amplification», in his book of «*The Acquired Knowledge Concerning the Cultivation of Gold*» (in Arabic: *al-ʿIlm al-muktasab fi zirāʿat aḏ- ḏahab),* pp. 55–57.

3.2. Amplification of Material Aspects

If choice is possible, the material is the first choice the author of a picture makes. And this can already tell us something.

Now we will look just at a few materials with which a picture can be created. They serve as examples for all the other materials.

a. Sheet

The quality of the chosen sheet of paper reflects the value given to an image that comes up from the depth. As already mentioned, there are *always* two possibilities for the interpretation of each such criterion. If, for example, somebody chose toilet paper, this could point to the low value being given to what is painted. *But* it could also be a hint about the painter's ability to let collective values go and make the lowest material the carrier for the soul's symbolic expressions.

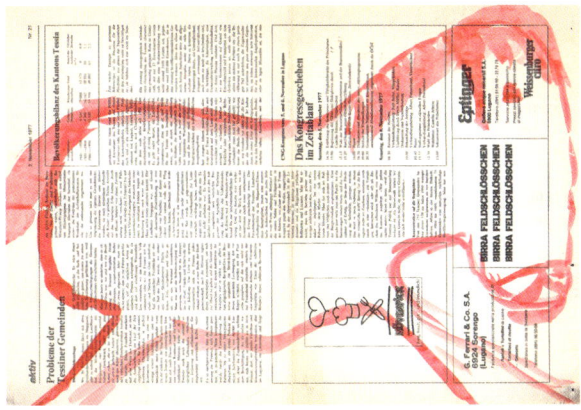

Fig. 33: Picture painted by a 51-year-old woman. The use of this sort of sheet (newspaper) could point either to a very spontaneous decision to bring the represented emotion, a red horse as she called it, into a form. But it could also point to the low value that is given to the animal drive. We will come back to this picture later (see also Fig. 94 on p. 119).

b. Medium

If the picture is created using a specific medium, and again, *if* there was a possibility for a choice, we can amplify on the meaning of the medium. We will first look at the characteristics of the different media and then make the step towards a psychological statement. This is the main procedure which we will apply to each aspect considered for interpretation. Which one of the different ways of understanding each criterion is the correct one depends entirely on the context of the picture we look at. It will emerge during the work of interpretation.

PENCIL
Characteristics: It can be erased and it has no colour of its own. With these traits, however, there are also huge varieties of possible nuances, if we think for instance of Albrecht Dürer's pencil drawings.
Psychological interpretation: The use of pencil can point either to an author who is not yet committed to the content of the picture, avoiding «confessing colour» (as we say in German) and keeping control over emotions out of fear of a confrontation with the reality of the psychic background. *But,* depending on the whole context, the medium pencil can also point to a concentration on the main features of what should be represented and a care for its precise shaping in an effort to create a picture as close as possible to an image from the inner world (see Fig. 34).

INK
Characteristics: Unlike pencil, ink is not easy to correct. It is flowing, and the black-white allows fine nuances and moods to become visible, like on a black-and-white photograph.
Psychological interpretation: The author does not «confess any colour». There can be a hard contrast between black and white. *But* this can also point to a concentration on the main features of the theme paired with the courage to let the inner forces flow and to let things happen. In Japanese ink painting, this art has developed into a Zen way (see Fig. 93 on p. 118).

COLOURED PENCIL
Characteristics: The picture becomes colourful, but it can also be hard, brittle and dry. On the other hand, this medium can also lead to very fine, intensively elaborated and differentiated pictures (see Fig. 35).

Amplification of Material Aspects

Fig. 34: Picture drawn by a 38-year-old man. This was done at the beginning of his analysis, to show me his situation. Pencil used as the medium points on the one hand to the fear of showing emotions and losing control of a precise drawing. But on the other hand this could also point to the need to creating as precise an image as possible, with the possibility of erasing first attempts. We will come back to this picture later (see also Fig. 90 on p. 114).

Fig. 35: Coloured pencil picture by a 45-year-old woman. Spontaneous expression of very strong feeling towards an unknown other living entity in her soul. The continous and faithful relationship to this other world led to completely unexpected discoveries of inner treasures (see also Fig. 62 on p. 83).

Psychological interpretation: The picture is colourful and brings in the emotional background. But it is still quite controlled. This can point to a careful presentation of something emotional *but* it can also point to ambivalence between «confessing colour» and controlling the emotion at the same time.

FINGER PAINT

Characteristics: This is a medium that can be used quite spontaneously. It is a medium favoured by little children. Differentiated colouring is not easily possible. The fingers of the author are expressing themselves directly in the picture.

Psychological interpretation: It is a direct spontaneous expression of emotions, *but* it can also point to a still quite undifferentiated emotionality (see Fig. 36 and 37).

Fig. 36: First spontaneous yet encouraged attempt to express a highly charged mouse-phobia in a picture (see also Fig. 15 on p. 34).

Fig. 37: First attempt to use colour by the man who drew figure 34. Spontaneous expression of emotions is met by an extremely well-structured grid of black lines.

BALLPOINT PEN

Characteristics: The ballpoint pen is a frequently-used writing tool, practical and functional. It is good for making clear lines but rather difficult to use for filling out space with colour.

Psychological interpretation: The pictures made with ballpoint pen can point to a dry, sober, cold or even sloppy expression *or* to a spontaneous, clear, matter-of-fact, down-to-earth, clearly determined expression.

WATERCOLOUR

Characteristics: This medium is by nature flowing, running often in a surprisingly unexpected way. It is difficult to correct watercolour and the background is strongly involved in the way the picture comes out.

Psychological interpretation: This medium allows nuances on the emotional level. It needs openness towards the spontaneous happenings of objective psyche. *But*, on the other hand, it can also mirror an undetermined attitude, characterized by dreaminess and a too-weak ego (Fig. 38 and 39).

Fig. 38: Spontaneous painting of a landscape by a 27-year-old man with a problem of gender identity. The opposites of land, sea and heaven are misty.

Fig. 39: Picture by a 28-year-old woman, showing great care to express the emotional impact that this snake had on her.

OIL PAINT

Characteristics: Working with this medium needs quite an effort. One has to learn the art of oil painting. It allows a very differentiated expression and, unlike with watercolour, correction is quite easy.

Psychological interpretation: This medium can reflect a deep involvement of the author with what is represented—only the very best is good enough, so to speak. *Or* it can point to an attitude that wants to control, hide, repress and censor with perfection.

MIXTURE OF DIFFERENT MODES OF EXPRESSION

Characteristics: When we find, for instance, pencil and watercolour used together in a picture, we may understand such a combination of two media by amplification of each one of them and then by combining the two, again looking at the interpretation in two ways.

Psychological interpretation: The combination of pencil and watercolour may point to a disagreement or ambivalence between controlling (pencil) and letting things flow (watercolour). *But,* on the other hand, this combination could also point to some special care that is given to what is represented, in order to express the complementary modes of the psyche.

Fig. 40: Picture by a 27-year-old man. The pencil used together with watercolour points here rather to the author's ambivalence between the pencil, which allows clearly defined forms on the one hand, and the spontaneous flow of watercolour on the other hand (see also Fig. 150 on p. 166).

c. Frame

A strong frame is an element of order and can point to a fearful, rigid, confining attitude towards the content of the picture. *But* it can also point to something highly treasured within the frame, something that needs to be strongly protected.

The complete lack of a frame can point to a state of being overwhelmed by the content that cannot be contained in a frame. This is especially the case when there are motifs that are cut by the edge of the paper. It could be a sign that ego consciousness no longer was the structuring centre in the process of creating the picture, pointing to a weak ego or worse to a schizoid structure. *But* it can also mean that for the time being, the represented content is too huge and numinous to be understood within the present conscious frame of the author.

d. Format

A very *large-sized* picture can point to the great importance and value of what is represented. *But* it can also be an expression of a tendency to grandiosity, exaggeration or hybris.

A very *small size* on the other side can point to a contemptuous, fearful or modest attitude towards what comes up from the inner world of dream and fantasy. *But* it can also reflect an intensity of something precious as we can see, for instance, in Persian miniatures.

In a series of created pictures a remarkable *change of size* can point to an unsteady and restless ambivalent person, for instance swinging between a feeling of grandiosity and inferiority, *or* it could mirror the need to focus and enlarge periodically one's view of certain aspects, in order to see clearer and then again not to lose sight of the greater context.

The *difference between a portrait format or a landscape format* is a further valuable criterion for the understanding of a picture. We can understand these two formats in their archetypal meaning, if we consider that they both deviate in a certain way from the square (see Fig. 41).

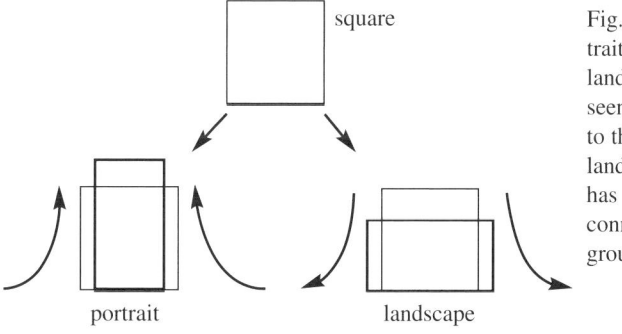

Fig. 41: The portrait format and the landscape format seen in relationship to the square. The landscape format has relatively more connection with the ground.

The square represents a perfectly balanced order between any type of opposites (expressed in the horizontal and the vertical lines): body and spirit, earth and sky, time and space, etc. It is from this static order that the two formats move into one or the other opposing direction.

Portrait format: This can be understood as a striving for spiritualization or greater depth, for the search to distill the meaning out of a concrete situation. We are reminded of pictures by El Greco or of the Gothic style. *But* it can also point to an attempt to escape from the hard facts of reality and thus this shows a tendency to lose contact with the ground.

Landscape format: This format is strongly connected to the ground. We can think of pictures of Rubens or of the Renaissance in general, the time when the value of mother earth was rediscovered in Europe. *But* on the other hand, this format can also point to a contact with mother earth where the predominance of the horizontal over the vertical indicates that the ego-consciousness is uppermost, thus entailing a loss of height.[2]

A *change of portrait format to landscape format* in a series of pictures can in general point to a change of attitude or to a new quality of the content. It can be understood as either a transformation from a more spiritual attitude towards the represented content to a realization in the here and now. *But* it can also point to a loss of a more spiritual attitude and an entanglement in concretisation.

Fig. 42: The change from portrait format to landscape format in a series of pictures.

If we find a *change from landscape format to portrait format,* that can point to an acquiring of a more symbolic or spiritual attitude towards a concrete situation or motive; *or* the same fact could mirror an attempt to get away from the facts of the reality of life that are, at that time at least, too difficult to deal with.

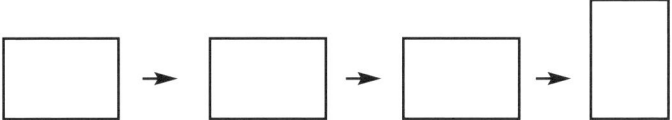

Fig. 43: The change from landscape format to portrait format in a series of pictures.

---

[2] C.G. Jung, *Psychology and Alchemy* [Coll. Works 12], § 287.

3.3. Formal Aspects
a. Organization

Organization or order is the opposite pole to chaos. There are basically two ways of ordering things. One is in accordance with the constellation in the unconscious and the other is not in accordance with it. Different elements can bring order to a picture, for instance symmetries, central perspective and grids. According to the relationship of the order-giving elements with the other elements of the picture, we can figure out whether the given order is, or is not, in accordance with the unconscious.

ORDER IN ACCORDANCE WITH THE UNCONSCIOUS
Such an order gives the impression of being coherent and adequate, as all the different elements seem to be properly related to each other. It mirrors an ego that does not need to defend itself by excluding something unacceptable from the inner world. *But* such an organization in a picture can also be a compensation from the unconscious for a chaotic state existing at the conscious level. This can be seen especially well in the apparition of a so-called mandala (Sanskrit: circle) that protects the individual personality. A mandala is like a magic charm by which the unconscious suggests a new conscious attitude that is again in tune with the wholeness of the psychic background (see Fig. 127 on p. 148). The first forms of mandalas already appear in children's paintings in connection with the birth of individual consciousness[3].

ORDER NOT IN ACCORDANCE WITH THE UNCONSCIOUS
By such an order we understand a structure of a picture that gives the impression of needing to keep rigid order as a result of fear, obsession or compulsion. This kind of order looks stiff, tight, rigid, and controlling. Fences, nets, grids can point to such a fear coming from an autonomous content. As such an expression of a rigid order mirrors an ego-consciousness that only represents a part of the psyche: such order points to the need for a renewal of the general attitude of the ego (see Fig. 45). *But* on the other

---

[3] Rhoda Kellog showed this in her collection of paintings done by 3- to 4-year-old children. See R. Kellog, *Finger Painting in the Golden Gate Nursery School*.

70 Formal Aspects

hand this sort of order can also mirror a legitimate, life-saving control against some overwhelming unconscious content (see also Fig. 45).

LITTLE OR NO ORGANIZATION

This can point to a «letting-go of ego control» at the time when an entry into the depth of the unconscious is taking place. *Or* it could point to a lack of a solid ego, where the mixture of the opposites is dominant. This can go so far

Fig. 44 (above): Hardly any organization, pointing to a rather weak ego structure that cannot protect against an overflow from the unconscious (see also Fig. 38).

Fig. 45 (left): Extremely strong organization, needed to control a first trial to allow colours to appear (see also Fig. 37).

Fig. 46: Order that appears to be in accordance with the content, emerging out of a black depression (see also Fig. 139).

as to be an overflow from the unconscious with a danger of dissociation. Chaos and order can both emerge from the unconscious (see Fig. 44).

b. Proportion

Proportion tells us where the energy lies and how things are related to each other. We can see that in a simple and clear way when we look at architecture. In former times, the church, temple or mosque used to be the tallest building in a settlement. That has now changed, mirroring the general secularisation of our time (see Fig. 47).

We can look at the relationship or proportion of the picture sheet to the medium, the technique to the medium, the motif to the format (landscape or portrait and size), the motifs to other motifs, the colours to space symbolism etc.

Fig. 47: Mosque in Cairo. Proportion tells us where the energy lies and how things are related to each other, also in the outer secularized world. The text on the minaret reads «Allah is great».

In general we can say that what is big is what is important to me or what irritates or frightens me. Proportion is quite an important and extremely helpful criterion, used widely in graphology and in different tests, such as the tree test.[4]

Fig. 48: Drawn by a 42-year-old woman.   Fig. 49: Painted by a 26-year-old woman.

Proportion of format and motif: We look now at an example of a single big tree (Fig. 48), squeezed into a landscape format. The spiritual life of this person would need a format adequate to the vertical growth of the tree. The tree in figure 49 is joined with the proper portrait format. Psychologically figure 48 would point to a limiting framing of unconscious forces by the ego, which could inhibit its proper growth. By that the further unfolding of the spiritual dimension of life, which is symbolized here by the crown of the tree, would be limited. *But* the same picture could also mirror a conflict between the hard reality of life's demands that limits the growth of the tree into the vertical height and depth.

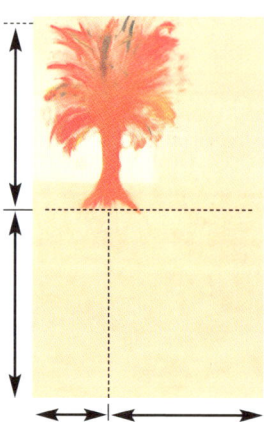

Fig. 50: Proportion of a motif to space symbolism.

Figure 50 is modified on a computer. It shows how one can ask the picture what it wants to say if this tree were in the upper left corner, using up (in size) only half the height of the paper. We will look later at the symbolism of the space in detail. What we could say in this modified example is that obviously the upper left quadrant of the given space absorbs in a possessive way all the energy of that person, leaving

---

[4]   See K. Koch, *Der Baumtest. Der Baumzeichenversuch als psychodiagnostisches Hilfsmittel.*

the rest of the space unused. *But,* on the other hand, it could also point to a need to concentrate all the energy of the tree in this area because it is the only 'soil' where the tree can grow for the time being.

Fig. 51: The "Two Women" by a 35-year-old engineer mirrors a split image of the feminine: On the upper half of the picture we see a big daemonic head with an asexual tiny body and geometrical figures around it. On the lower half, under water —in the unconscious—we see a woman with huge thighs and a tiny head. She is surrounded by lush green sea plants. This picture shows, in a nutshell, that things regarding the feminine are really out of proportion: some rational, devouring, intellectual view of the feminine in the 'upper floor' and concentration just on the body in the unconscious. (Picture from J. Jacobi, *Vom Bilderreichtum der Seele,* p. 72; see also Fig. 77 on p. 97).

c. Movement

We look for movement in a picture, as this gives us hints about where and how strongly the energy of the author is flowing at that time. Movement is an expression of emotion that comes from the Latin word *movere* = to move. Lines, forms, motifs or colours can indicate movement.

Movement always points to the future. A movement to the left side of the picture points to a development that goes either towards introversion in order to retrieve things lost in the past *or* to a regression that can lead to a getting stuck in resentment. A movement that tends to the right side of the picture can either point to a flow and development in the outer world (see Fig. 53) *or* to a thoughtless, meaningless extraversion.

The movement in a picture gives us prognostic hints: In which direction does the energy flow? *Or:* What could be the next step in the process? All the movement in figure 59 on page 80 for instance, is directed to the centre of the picture, the «sleeping beauty» in the transparent magic wand.

Clockwise movement: This can point to the consolidation of a centre 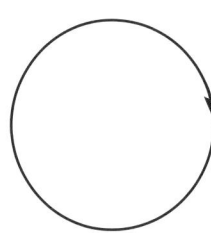 or to a progression in consciousness. As we can see all over the world, the circumambulation of holy places like shrines, temples or mountains practically always goes clockwise. This also has to do with the right hand that is thus always to the side of the holy centre. In all societies, the right hand has been known as the «clean» hand, the one used for eating. This clockwise movement can be considered also as the origin of the fact that all the clocks in the world turn clockwise. *But* the clockwise movement can also point to a mechanical routine and thus to the petrification of what is in the centre.

Counter-clockwise movement: In a counter-clockwise movement around a centre, one has the left hand, the «dirty» hand, towards the centre. 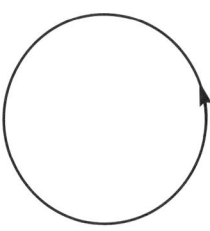 The aim of this counter-clockwise movement is the regeneration of a central divine image that is no longer visible or living.[5] This counter-clockwise movement is thus turning towards the unconscious, to death and resurrection and to the creation of a new symbol. *But* this movement can also point to the danger of being lost in the abyss of the unconscious, being unable to find the redeeming centring symbol.

---

[5] Tantric Yoga, for instance, is called the path of the left hand. See also the alchemical picture series of the *Rosarium*, discussed by C.G. Jung in: *Psychology of Transference* [Coll. Works 16], § 410.

Formal Aspects

Fig. 52: By the same person as for figure 45 on page 70. The order is less rigid, the colours are no longer in clearly divided compartments. But no movement is visible.

Fig. 53: By the same person as for figure 52. Here we can see a clear movement from left to right. The yellow circle changes into a blue one, which then enters the black, the darkness of the night—for the necessary change of the old light or «clear-cut» world view of this successful 38-year-old business manager. This transformation went on to lead to a renewal of consciousness (see also Fig. 105 on p. 131).

3.4. Space Symbolism
a. The Quality of Location

Space symbolism is based on collective human experience and can be checked—like every other criterion of picture interpretation—by an empiric approach. An empty sheet is never just an empty space. It is immediately conditioned by our perception, filled with our archetypal experience of space. The left side is related to the sinister, the dark side and the past, while the right side is connected to the bright side and the future.[6] In the same way the upper part is connected to elevation, spirit and growing-up, while the bottom is connected to ground, roots and grounding.

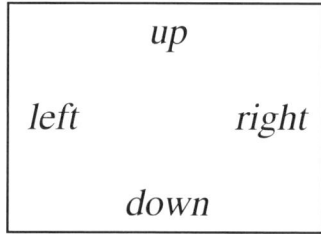

Fig. 54: The empty sheet is never just an empty space. It is immediately filled with our archetypal experience of space.

The left–right symbolism can be explained by the following fact: the movement from left to right seems to be connected to the *development in time* for human beings all over the world. Even languages that are written from right to left, as is the case with Arabic or Chinese, the numbers 1 2 3 4 5 ... are written from left to right. In the northern hemisphere where all high cultures originate, the sun and all 'sky-bodies' travel from the left to the right, due to the rotatation of the earth. On the other hand, we all experience growth on earth connected to «growing up», that is from down below, upwards. This provides the basis for understanding the archetypal dimension of space symbolism.

---

[6] See for instance K. Koch, *Der Baumtest. Der Baumzeichenversuch als Psycho-diagnostisches Hilfsmittel*. (This is a more systematic and detailed later work of Koch's, who presented his earlier results in *The Tree Test. The tree-drawing test as an aid in Psycho-diagnosis*, which has not yet been translated into English).

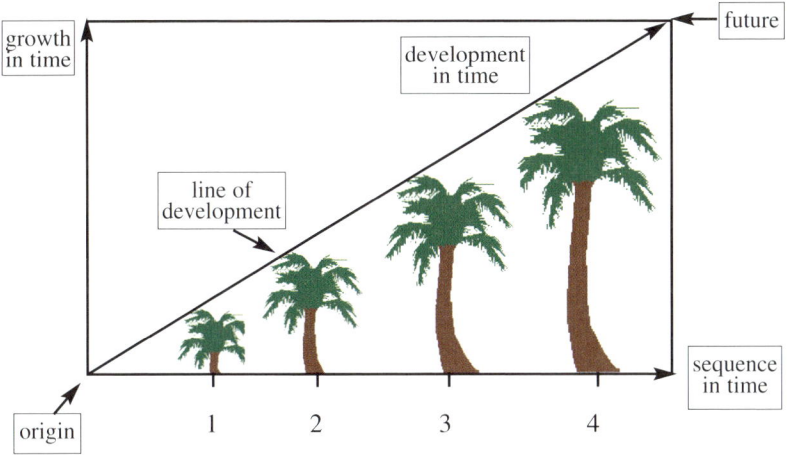

Fig. 55: The stages of the growth of the tree (1–4) show the development in time, from left to right and upwards. This gives the line of development that is projected unconsciously onto the empty sheet, as made evident in the coin test devised by Michael Grünwald.

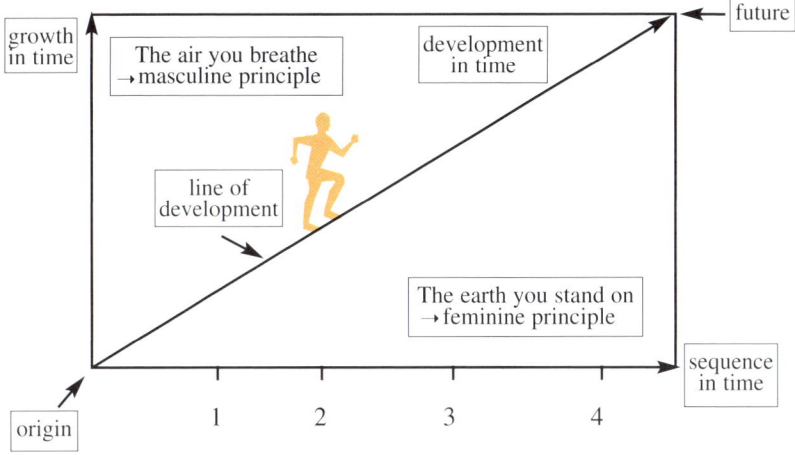

Fig. 56: The line of development divides the sheet into the "air" one breathes and the "earth" one stands on, the masculine and the feminine principle.

A test developed by Michael Grünwald, shows that our perception of an empty sheet is really structured in this archetypal way.[7] The test-person is asked to put a coin (as a symbol of that person) on an empty white sheet in landscape format (a symbol of one's life), in the place where he or she thinks they are standing now. Then a second coin is given with the question: «Put the coin where you think you will be standing in ten years' time». And a third coin with the words: «Put the coin where you think you were standing ten years ago». Four out of five persons who were tested in this way had laid the three coins in such a way that they formed a line that was close to the above-mentioned development line (see Fig. 55 and 56).

Fig. 57: Woodcarving by a 24-year-old man who saw this carving in a dream. This vision impressed the dreamer so much that he created this wooden plate. It shows a strong diagonal line to the upper right-hand corner, suggesting the possibility of or need for the development of the human figure in the lower right-hand corner. This human figure is made up of a head (the sun) and a torso made up of a series of crescent moons. In the course of this journey upward, the figure passes six «milestones», marked with the symbols of the six planets, as was clear in the dream. The symbol of the union of the sun and moon indicates that the bipolar self not only wants but needs to become conscious. This journey through the planets forced him to reassess his world view by being confronted with the archetypal background of his soul.

---

[7] It is one of ten tests developed by Michael Grünwald. See K. Koch, *Der Baumtest*, p. 33.

In order to find a connection to space symbolism it is recommendable to mentally apply a horizontal or—if more appropriate to the specific character of the picture—a diagonal grid on to the picture. The shaded areas show the parts of the sheet that relatively represent the unconscious part of the psyche.[8] The two grids placed above each other show the archetypal «brightest and darkest parts» of a sheet.

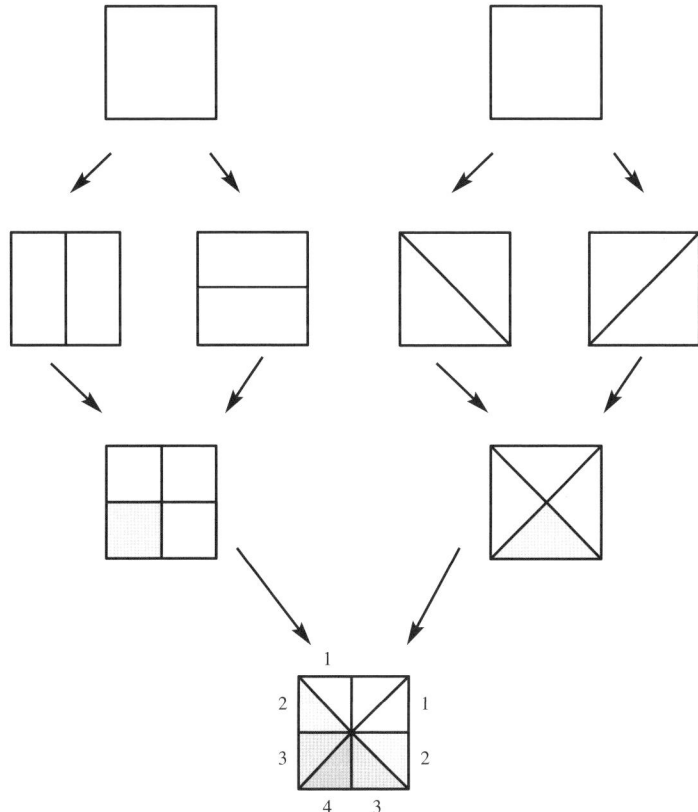

Fig. 58: The archetypal darkest and the brightest parts of space.

---

[8] Whenever we are confronted with a portrait, space symbolism has to be inverted from left to right and vice versa.

Inverting a picture can show the importance of a space symbolism. For example it would make quite a difference to see this same picture—which we could call «Sleeping beauty in the transparent magic wand»—the other way round! In the inverted picture on the right, the central content of the picture gives a sense of blocking the line of development instead of leading to the future.

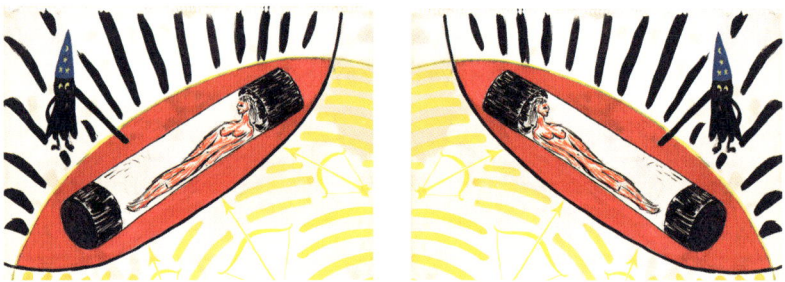

Fig. 59: Inversion of Fig. 143 on page 161.

b. Perspective

Perspective tells us how the author sees what is represented. An overview of the history of the way perspective was applied gives us a better understanding of its symbolism.

In ancient Egyptian paintings we find mainly a so-called *aspective*, meaning that we are given a front view of the important aspects. For instance the eye is represented in front view, in spite of its general view being a side one. What is considered important is represented in its most powerful and clear appearance (see Fig. 60).

Looking at paintings from ancient Greek and Roman times, we find the various elements of a picture in simple juxtaposition, that is one placed next to the other. This practice continued up until the Middle Ages, when perspective was mainly given by colour and light. Only in the period of the Renaissance did the central perspective become a main feature. It expressed a new discovery of the human dimension on earth, where human beings were stating: «This is the way *I* see that scene». It meant quite a strengthening of the ego. In modern times, Cubism again dissolved all perspective, mirroring the relativity of the human ego in this world. From this we can see that the change of perspective reflects a change of worldview.[9]

---

[9] I owe these reflections to Dr P. Brutsche's diploma thesis at the C.G. Jung Institute, *Die Psychologische Bedeutung der Perspektive in Analysandenzeichnungen.*

Space Symbolism

Fig. 60: Aspective view of trees, standing around a pond. The aspect, which for the Ancient Egyptians was considered important, was represented in its most powerful and clear appearance: the pond is seen from above, the different trees are shown from the side. Papyrus from the book of the dead of Nakht, Thebes, New Kingdom, 18th dynasty, around 1300 BC. This part of the vignette shows Nakht venerating Osiris.

When in a picture series a *development of central perspective* becomes apparent, this can point to the strengthening of the ego-complex that allows a further encounter with the unconscious. *But* it could also mirror a growing control of what is represented.

On the other hand, we can say that the *decrease in perspective* in a series of pictures can point to a loosening of ego-control with a readiness to accept whatever new comes from the inner world. In this way the ego is no longer defined by exclusion. *But* it could also mirror dissolution of the ability to order what is represented in the picture.

Light perspective can mirror an ego too weak to hold the tension of the opposites *or* it can point to a state where the foreground and the background are not divided by a defined perspective, giving a possibility for the appearance of a reconciling symbol.

Central and linear perspective needs to be constructed. It is easier for the thinking function to cope with this sort of perspective. It was well developed at the time of the Renaissance. It points to a good sense of reality *or* being bogged down in the concrete.

Sometimes we find in a picture an *incoherence of the perspective,* something like a tectonic rupture. That can point to a borderline or a psychotic structure *or* to a deep inner psychic inconsistency.

No perspective in a picture can point to a lack of depth and knowledge of a shadow side of life, as for instance the shadow of one's own ego-consciousness. *Or* it can mean an abstraction from the three-dimensional reality to come to the essence of things, as shown for example in a mandala.

We now want to see what space symbolism can contribute to the understanding of a picture. Following is a picture by a 26-year-old teacher, who brought me this illustration of his situation (see Fig. 61). He suffered from a conflict between his spiritual aspirations and the dull demands of everyday life. We see him—as if on stage—in front of something like a stone, which is wrapped up in a blue–red ribbon. He holds an enormous sword towards a pool of snakes, as if to defend himself with it. In the background to the right we see dark clouds like those before a thunderstorm, under which there is a yellow ribbon of what could be called the sunshine behind the clouds. If we focus on the space symbolism and the perspective, we could say that the image illustrates the unsolvable conflict in the foreground: the ego heroically tries to fight the snakes that would be the frightening aspects coming from the unconscious. But there is a clear perspective or way out of the unsolvable conflict: why not just move around the snakes «on the natural development line»? This development of consciousness led the man finally to life, marriage and unexpected creativity that brought a reconciliation of his bewildering snake-world with his quest for meaning.

Fig. 61: Picture by a 26-year-old man.

Fig. 62: Picture by a 49-year-old woman. The panther can be understood as a wild and strong drive-energy that carries with its yellow eyes the possibility of light and insights. The picture shows the animal related to the moon and the sea on the left and to the red amarylis on the right. The moon as the archetypal symbol for relatedness and eros is the more unconscious background of this energy, while the flower is the more human expression of this devilish-black light-bringer (Lucifer). The cross in the middle is an emerging uniting symbol.

3.5. Colour Symbolism

a. Basic Aspects

Colours express and induce feelings, moods and emotions. They are a symbol of life «in all its colours». The colours around us influence our state of being, and the colours we wear often express the way we feel at any given moment. It is known that every human has his or her favourite colours, as the Swiss psychologist Max Lüscher was able to make evident in his research. The so-called Lüscher colour test is based on this fact.[10] He was also able to prove that the way people react to colours is independent of age, gender and culture.

There is a significant amount of literature on colours and colour symbolism that deals with the relationship of colour and psyche. Every lexicon of symbols offers amplification material for the different colours. And there are different books containing interesting amplifications of the different colours, quoting artists, poets, myths and fairy tales from different cultures, relating this to psychic states and development as well as to body parts.[11] Avoid overdoing the study of such collections of amplifications. By going too much into detail one can easily get lost, «unable to see the wood for the trees».

The aim here instead is to amplify the different colours in a concise way, just as far as is necessary for the interpretation of pictures. It is important that the basic amplifications of the different elements of a picture *really stay with us,* that they don't have to be learnt by heart, so to speak. Only if we feel at home with the archetypal meaning of the different colours—and other criteria—will we enjoy the art of picture interpretation and only with this motivation will we continue to practise it. And the more we practise, the more we will enjoy it. For that reason we will also «keep it simple and straight» with colours.

There are some remarkable features about colours. Let us first look at the physical facts, how they were presented in an experiment by Isaac Newton in 1676. He demonstrated that a triangular prism can break up

---

[10] See M. Lüscher, *The Lüscher Colour Test.*
[11] See for instance I. Riedel's book on colour symbolism: *Farbsymbolik.*

white sunlight into the colours of the rainbow, starting with red, then orange, yellow, green, blue and finally ending with violet. He named this phenomenon the spectrum (see Fig. 63).

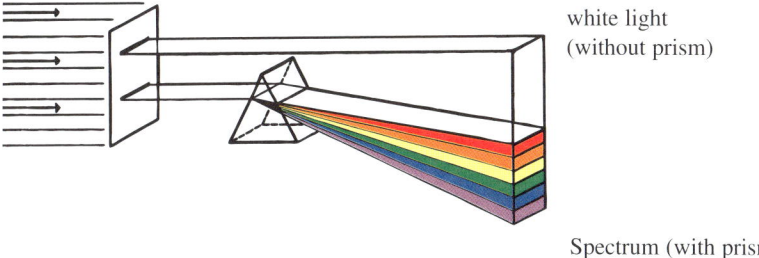

Fig. 63: The splitting up of white sunlight into different colours, as demonstrated by an experiment of Isaac Newton in 1676.

J.W. Goethe, in his *Farbenlehre* (finished in 1808), rejected in sharp polemic the analytic and quantitative approach of Newton, defending instead the holistic view of the artist and the feeling aspect of colour. Among many other things he arranged the six colours of the rainbow on a circle, discussing the harmonies of colours on this basis (see Fig. 64).

Goethe also tried to find ways to connect colours to the typology of

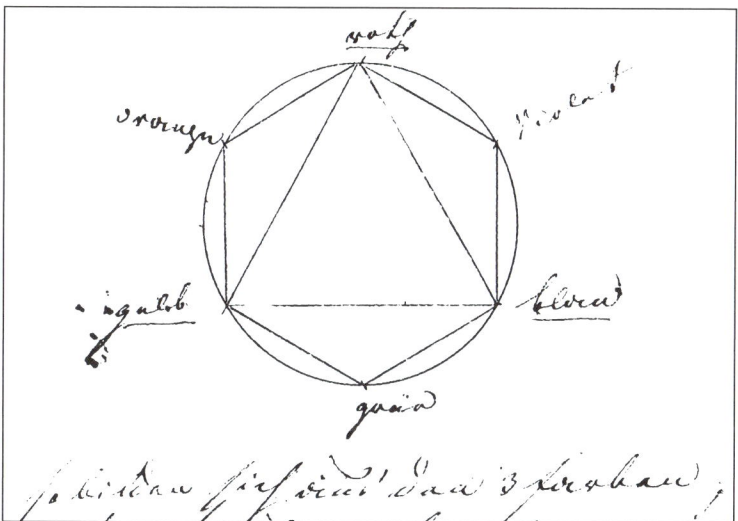

Fig. 64: The colours of the rainbow, arranged on a circle by J.W. Goethe. From O. Krätz (ed.), *Goethe und die Naturwissenschaften*, p. 174.

humans as can be seen from the following picture that was the basis for an intensive discussion with Friedrich Schiller (see Fig. 65).

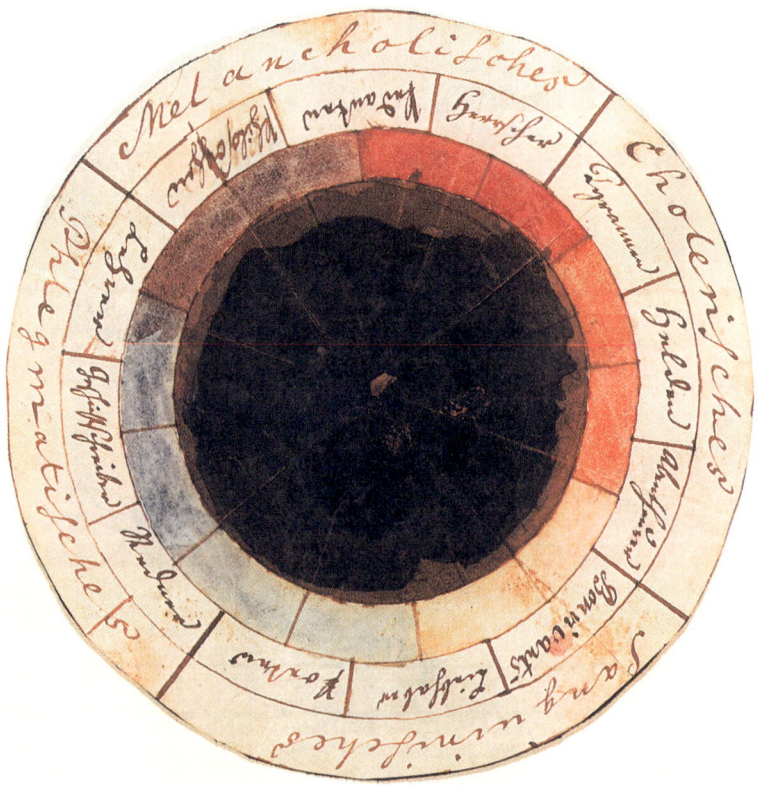

Fig. 65: The circle of the colours in relationship to the four temperaments. The writing on this picture is F. Schiller's.[12]

In order to get acquainted with the symbolism of the six colours of the rainbow, it is helpful to follow Goethe's reflections. These six colours can be divided into three basic colours (red, blue and yellow) and three mixtures of these basic colours (green, orange and violet). The three basic colours can be arranged on a circle, as shown in figure 66.

[12] O, Krätz (ed.), *Goethe und die Naturwissenschaften*, p. 172.

Colour Symbolism

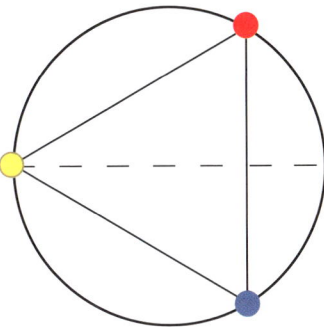

Fig. 66: The three basic colours arranged on a circle.

In between the basic colours we have the mixture of these colours. Again arranged on a circle we get the following sequence, which brings all the colours of the rainbow into view (see Fig. 67).

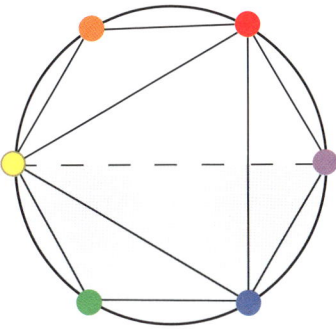

Fig. 67: The six colours of the rainbow can be arranged on a circle and connected to the changing qualities of the sun, as a symbol of human consciousness.

The arrangement of the sequence yellow, orange, red, violet, blue and green in the way given above (Fig. 67) allows a comparison with the course of the sun. This has proved to be a helpful analogy. The inspiration to do this came to me from two sources: first from a text by an Arab alchemist, who connected the six colours of the rainbow to different psychic states.[13] And second from my work with the Pharaonic books of the afterlife, where the journey of the sun god through the hours of the day and the night is described.[14] Thus, when we connect the colours of the rainbow to the changing qualities of the sun, which is a symbol of human consciousness, we get a basic idea of the psychic quality of each colour (see Fig. 68). The warm «extraverted» colours are in the upper part while the cold «introverted» colours are in the lower part. Yellow and violet are in between. And in the same way as the sun first increases its intensity and decreases after midday, the colours of the spectrum also heat up to orange–red and then calm down to violet, while the lower half of the circle the colours become more calm and cool, turning to blue. And as the new day is born at midnight, the colours increase in warmth and «extraverted intensity» after the blue–green, arriving at the green and finally rising up to the yellow, the emerging light. Of course this is only an analogy as the sun in fact mostly rises as a red–orange fireball.

The Complementary Colours
We have seen on page 85 (Fig. 63) that white light can be split up into different colours by a prism, creating the six colours of the rainbow that in figure 68 are arranged on a circle. If we choose from these colours on the circle those two colours which are opposed to each other as light beams and add them to each other, for example the red and the green, the resulting light will be white again, like the original light that was sent through the prism. We call those two sorts of lights, which together make up white, complementary colours. Therefore we say that red and green, blue and orange, yellow and violet are complementary to each other.

Our Procedure
When focusing on the colour symbolism in a picture it can be quite helpful to see which colours are missing, in order to draw greater attemtion to those which are present.

We will now amplify the different basic colours, first from the point of view of the archetypal experience that comes from contact with nature. Then we will also look at some popular statements, mythological motifs and at some facts from the natural sciences. We will start with the basic colours red, blue, and yellow then continue with the mixed colours of the spectrum, green, orange and violet. Finally we will turn to some other important colours: brown, black, grey and white.

---

[13] M. Ibn Umail, *The Book of the Explanations of the Symbols*, p. 11, line 13f.
[14] See Th. Abt and E. Hornung, *Knowledge for the Afterlife*.

Fig. 68: The circle of the colours split again from six into twelve colours. The opposing colours are always complementary.[15]

---

[15] From J. Itten, *Kunst der Farbe,* p. 31. The picture here has been rotated clockwise by 90 degrees in order to have yellow on the left side.

b. The Three Basic Colours (Red, Blue, Yellow)

RED

The most common and emotionally strong human experiences of red down on earth are blood and glowing fire. Blood connects red to life, biological drives, emotions, feelings of love and hatred, passion, sensuality and sex; while the red of the glowing fire associates red with warmth but also with destructive heat.

In the animal kingdom red is a so-called signal colour, attracting for instance the attention of animals, mostly mammals, to certain parts of the body for mating. For humans, too, red triggers off emotions of love. But red can also ward off or evoke aggression. It is a well-known revolutionary colour, or again, it is the colour of the traffic light sign accepted worldwide for «stop!».

In popular belief in the Western world, the devil is associated with red as he is the master of fire, passions, desirousness etc. This sinful aspect of red in effect splits human beings off from the good Lord in heaven. But on the other hand, red is also the colour of love, the force that can unite the opposites. For the old Romans, both the goddess of love, Venus, and the god of war, Mars, were connected to red.

SUMMARY OF THE TWO SIDES OF RED:	
+	–
warmth	burning heat
uniting (Venus)	dividing (Mars, devil)
renewing	destroying

Red can be understood in general as a vitalizing warming-up colour that can bring life or destruction.

Fig. 69: [Above right.] Picture by a 37-year-old European woman. The picture shows the arising of a multi-armed, frightening, flaming figure that seems to emerge from the black below. The intensity of the red colour shows the strong emotion that is connected to this content. The figure reminds us of the multi-armed Hindu gods such as Siva or Kali-Durga, who are both life- and death-bringing deities. The green around the hands points to this life-bringing aspect. The gesture of the figure commands respect but also promises protection. This double aspect of the overwhelming energy of the lower, bodily realm was emerging in this woman and wanted to become conscious in its double aspect. The ten bunches of red hair of this figure could point to the spiritual wisdom that emerges from below.

Colour Symbolism

Fig. 69: Picture by a 37-year-old woman. (See also page 90.)

Fig. 70: Picture by a 26-year-old woman. The red sun before the horizon seriously threatened her situation. The cosmic order seems to be out of balance. It was important for her to recognize the danger but also not to panic and to know that such phenomena can occur at the time of complete renewal (see also Fig. 71).

Fig. 71: (See Fig. 70.) Seen in the light of alchemical symbolism, it seems to be an archetypal event that the sun, the fireball, must go down or be dissolved in order that the renewal of the personality can become possible. (From K.R.H. Frick, *Splendor Solis*, p. 179.)

BLUE

The most common and obvious experience of blue in nature comes from the sky. Whenever there are no clouds, the sky during day time appears blue to us. That colour blue gives humans the feeling of continuity. It also leads to a feeling of calmness, depth and breadth beyond any conscious understanding and thus leads to a sense of eternity. And, indeed, as has been tested out by different researchers, humans associate blue with peace, tranquillity, introversion, recovery, satisfaction, trust. In the Christian culture, the blue coat of mother Mary points to this protective aspect of the blue sky. But air, spirit, ice and coldness are also associated with blue.

Another common experience of blue is the water of the sea, river or lake; leading to associations of depth, width and the longing for our origin, the water out of which we all come.

There are some common sayings related to blue that further illustrate the symbolism of blue. In English we say «I am feeling blue», meaning I am sad or depressed. 'Blue-stocking' is a term for a woman who is too intellectual. Also in myth and fairy tales this relation of blue to the spirit is evident when we think of the blue flower or the blue light that has to be searched for. Natural science tells us that the blue waves are the higher energy-waves. In the colour spectrum they are on the ultra-violet side. Contrary to the warm red waves (on the infrared side of the spectrum) the blue waves are on the cold, «spiritual» side.

SUMMARY OF THE TWO SIDES OF BLUE:	
+	–
introversion	loss of reality
meaningful order	cold, rigid order
spirituality	spirit-possession
receptivity	possessive absorption

We can understand blue as the colour of receptivity and meaningful order *or* as rigid, possessive absorption.

Colour Symbolism

Fig. 72: Self-portrait by a 27-year-old woman in watercolour. The head shows an unprotected openness to the blue of the sky, to spiritual influences and opinions that are floating in the collective. Everything is nicely arranged in compartments and looks flat. The warm colours are all to the right, separated from the cold colours where we see her face.

Fig. 73: Picture by the same woman as for figure 72, produced about a year later. It shows the birth of a woman out of an egg in the depth of the blue and purple water. This birth from the water of the unconscious seems to take place in the warmth of the red and orange below the blue water. The woman who is born out of the egg can be understood as her true self no longer divided up into different compartments. The picture is a vision of what could emerge out of the unconscious by continuous loving warmth that is given to the potential Self in the depth of the psyche.

YELLOW

The most obvious experience of yellow is the sun. It reappears every day anew and rejuvenated. That mystery of renewal has inspired humans at all times in many parts of the world. It became a general symbol for human consciousness, which also rises every day fresh and renewed from sleep. But at night the moon and the stars appear yellow to us as well. These archetypal experiences of sun, moon and the stars connect yellow to light, and consciousness. But on the other hand, too much light can become destructive and dry everything up in the same way as the desert sun.

On a smaller scale, we commonly find urine and an unhealthy skin are yellow. This connects yellow also to some lower aspects of life. Yellow is also associated in popular belief with disease and cowardice.

But on earth, yellow is also associated with gold, that metal which, like the sun, is always constant and in many different cultures has become a symbol for the eternal inner psychic centre that—paradoxically—can make us conscious of both ourselves and itself.

SUMMARY OF THE TWO SIDES OF YELLOW:	
+	–
illuminating	life-destroying
redeeming	too much clarity
clarification	poisonous states

Yellow can be understood as colour that brings redeeming light *or* consciousness that can, however, also be life destroying.

Fig. 74: Picture by a 24-year-old woman with a mouse phobia. It shows an illuminating yellow mouse that is given a name. The ground is also partly coloured yellow as well as the sun. The picture had a redeeming effect. (See also Fig. 17 on p. 34.)

Colour Symbolism

Fig. 75: Picture by a 22-year-old man. Strong bright yellow strokes are found in the lower right and the upper left triangle. The same yellow is also the colour of the pupil of the daemonic one-eyed face and the circle (or ball) in the hands of the red man. Both are connected by a black line. The man suffered from an unexplainable overwhelming attraction to a woman that was for him—as a good friend of his put it—«like a fist in the eye». The yellow three strokes that come out of the lower left corner mirror the «sunny boy's» outer extraverted being. This is in strong contrast to the black landscape. The picture reveals that from the daemonic face comes a black landscape. A hidden autonomous complex, a «fiery daemonic other» is the source of his enigmatic compulsive attraction. That led the man to darkness, depression and introversion, but later also to the yellow treasure, the gold in the earth so to speak. (See also Fig. 86 on p. 105, where this picture is shown again.)

c. The Three Basic Mixed Colours (Green, Orange, Violet)

GREEN

The colour green is first of all seen in the green vegetation. Because of this it is associated with growth, with spring *but* also with suffocating, overgrowing vegetation and unripe fruit.

Among the different popular sayings, we find that in German, green represents hope, and yet, in English, there is the phrase «green with envy». In mythology, the gods of vegetation and resurrection, like Osiris, are green. Hermes-Thot, the father and guide of alchemy, is associated with the colour green. In the Koran, Chidr, the mysterious guide of Moses, is also green. The common association of green with the flow of life can also be found in the universal acceptance of green as the traffic-light signal for «Go!»

SUMMARY OF THE TWO SIDES OF GREEN:	
+	−
growth	overgrowth of vegetation
life-bringing	suffocating
hopeful	devouring

Green as the colour of vegetation symbolizes the renewing and flowing force of the unconscious. *But* green also points to the nourishing energy that can keep humans blissfully unconscious.

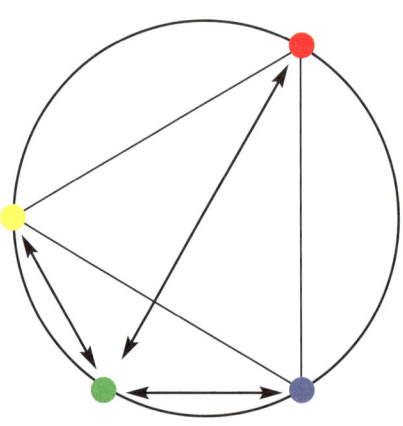

Fig. 76: Green is connected to all three basic colours. It is the mixture of yellow and blue and is the complementary colour of red.

Red is the complementary colour of green. That means, as we saw earlier, that green and red light together make up white light. Or, as experiments have shown, green light, when shone onto a white object, will cause the object to throw a red shadow.[16] This complementary aspect of green and red clarifies the quality of green. We understand red as a warm, vitalizing colour that can bring life or destruction. Green, as its complementary colour, contains what is completely missing in red: the qualities of the receptive blue and the light-giving yellow. Green points in this way to the mediating quality

---

[16] Experiments described by J. Itten, *Kunst der Farbe,* p. 82.

Colour Symbolism

of the spirit of vegetation, of «green Nature», which connects to all three basic colours. From this it becomes understandable why in alchemy green was the colour of the mediator Hermes.

Fig. 77: The green around the woman down below points to life-bringing quality that the bodily reality and attraction of the feminine thighs would carry for the 36-year-old painter. The «content in the green» would be the required complement to the devouring red of the frightening mouth of the upper woman (see also Fig. 51 on p. 73).

Fig. 78: Picture by a 34-year-old woman. Two fire-spitting green snakes are united in a mysterious way. The green snakes point to the living spirit of Nature that appears here in a bipolar form. The fire coming out of the snakes points to some fiery drive-energy that in the Christian context is associated with the devil. The image suggests that the two sides of this drive-energy can and must be seen now: its positive and negative, its active and receptive side. In such a balanced view, the spirit of the lower world can become a healing one, as is known from the symbol of two snakes of the caduceus of Hermes often seen outside pharmacies.

ORANGE

As a mixture of red and yellow, orange combines the characteristics of the luminous power of yellow and the vital energy and the warmth of red. The combination of red and yellow makes this colour fiery, lively, joyful and exciting, but it can also be irritating. A basic human experience of orange is the flame of the fire. For that reason, orange also has the quality of warmth, but it is also a signal colour, arousing attention and caution. That is why it became the colour accepted worldwide for the orange traffic-light, warning the driver that the signal is going change.

Orange is an energizing colour: it can activate, but also generate aggression; for the ancient Romans, orange was considered, like red, to be the colour of fiery Mars, their god of war and disharmony. But it is also a colour of union of two basic colours: red becomes spiritualised by yellow and, conversely, red warms up yellow. The clothes of Hindu monks (*sannyasins*) are orange, symbolizing the wisdom of a spiritualised passion.

SUMMARY OF THE TWO SIDES OF ORANGE:	
+	−
energizing	generating aggression
enlightening	creating disharmony
joyful, mediating	possessive, daemonic

Orange can be understood as a colour of energizing, joyful warm light *but* also of daemonic aggressiveness.

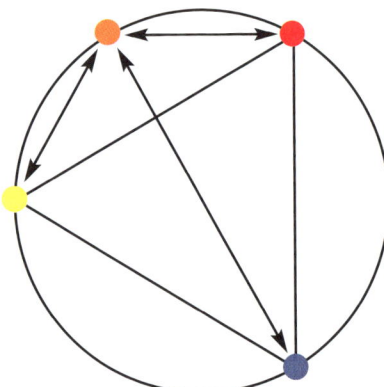

Fig.79: Orange is connected to all three basic colours.
It is the mixture of yellow and red, and its complementary colour is blue.

Orange is the complementary colour of blue. That clarifies the quality of orange in relation to the basic colours yellow, red and blue. We understood blue as the colour of receptivity and meaningful order or as mirror of rigid possessive absorption. In other words, blue is apart from light (yellow) and warmth (red). Orange, as its complement, carries what is missing in the blue: the qualities of the vitalizing, warm red and the enlightening yellow, which together make up the orange with the two sides it can point to. For all that, orange is also, as we have seen with green, a mediating colour, connecting to all three basic colours.

Fig. 80: Chalk-painting by a 26-year-old woman. The frightening fiery orange tree can point to a one-sided and unrooted isolation. But it can also point to a need for an understanding of the meaning of an overwhelming life energy. It became crucial in the work with this woman to reconnect her to her healthy archetypal background, the water and the earth of her unconscious. (See also Fig. 70, painted by the same woman.)

Violet

Being a mixture of the vitalizing warm red and spiritual cold blue, violet symbolizes the union of these extreme opposites of the spectrum. The union of the warm red and the cold blue in violet associates this colour with wholeness and completeness. This can point either to a mixture of the opposites or a union of the opposites, depending on the level of consciousness.

Fig. 81: The spectrum formed into a circle shows how violet unites its two ends, the blue and the red.

We can understand why violet, as the union of the extreme poles of the spectrum, is associated with the original mixture of opposites, to manipulating magic and losing one's solid standpoint by possession. On a higher level, however, violet points to the *mysterium coniunctionis*, to a union of the opposites of male and female and to highest spirituality in life—the union of humans with God.

The danger of a one-sided application of any symbolism became clear to me for the first time when I finished my diploma at the Jung Institute in 1975 and was invited immediately afterwards to the Leopold Szondi Institute to give an introduction to Jung's psychology. I organized a weekend in picture interpretation for the trainees. There we also worked out the amplifications of the colours. I must have unconsciously emphasized the quality of violet as being a mixture of opposites, without also pointing clearly to its other quality, which is the union of opposites. Next morning, everybody came for breakfast dressed in something violet. The devil knows where they got all those violet clothes from. We all had a good laugh.

SUMMARY OF THE TWO SIDES OF VIOLET:	
+	−
union of opposites	mixture of opposites
mediating	wishy-washy
spiritualizing	losing touch with reality

Violet expresses the union of the extremes of the spectrum, red and blue. *But* it can also point to an unhealthy mixture of the same opposites.

Colour Symbolism

The fact that violet is the complementary colour of yellow clarifies the quality of violet in relation to all the basic colours. The complement to yellow, which brings redeeming light or life-destroying consciousness, carries the qualities of the unconscious in its aspect of a mediating spirituality that comes from the earth and the sky at the same time.

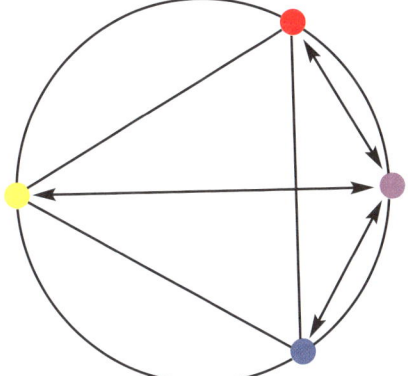

Fig. 82: Violet is connected to the three basic colours. It is the mixture of red and blue and the complementary colour of yellow.

Of the three mediating colours green is characterized by pointing to the *spirit of vegetation*—the green cells, so to speak. Energizing orange is connected to the *spirit that comes out of the bodily drives,* while violet is the *spirit that comes from below and above* at the same time.

Fig. 83: Picture by a 24-year-old man. It shows the invasion of a landscape with a red river by a violet daemonic witch, violet being here rather a mixture of opposites. On this witch sits a black blonde-haired, daemonic woman with bird's feet and four wings. It is an image that the man made in prison, awaiting a possible death sentence for the murder of his entire family.

d. Other Colours and Non-Colours

BROWN

Brown is not a colour of the spectrum, yet it is commonly found in nature, in fertile soil and dung, the very basis of all agriculture, which has contributed enormously to the development of human culture and consciousness.

The colour brown is most frequently experienced as earth, wood, bark and roots. This links the colour to life-supporting mother earth, to nourishing, protective and stabilizing matter (*materia* in Latin means wood). But brown is also experienced in the life-taking side of mother earth, in decaying leaves and plants. We also meet brown in smelly dung and faeces. These aspects link brown to decay and dirt—things normally rejected. «*In stercore invenitur aurum nostrum*» (in the dung-heap our gold is found) is a statement of the ancient alchemists. It expresses their experience that out of the decaying or rejected parts of the soul, the gold of the sages—consciousness—can be extracted.

These qualities of brown clarify its symbolic meaning. They point to the fertile basis of soil, matter and body: the basis of individual consciousness. *But,* on the other hand, brown is also connected to mud and stinking shit. That points to the motherly *massa confusa* at the beginning of the work, in which the ego can get stuck, being unable to unfold and develop in an independent and unique way.

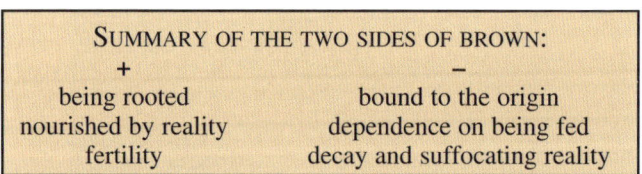

SUMMARY OF THE TWO SIDES OF BROWN:	
+	−
being rooted	bound to the origin
nourished by reality	dependence on being fed
fertility	decay and suffocating reality

Brown can be understood as the nourishing carrier of life that can, however, also have a regressive appeal.

Fig. 84 : Watercolour picture by a 27-year-old woman (see also Fig. 72 and 73). This picture is the fourth of a series following figure 73, the birth of a woman, her true self or a new consciousness, out of the egg. Here a bird is connected to a yellow triangle above and surrounded by brown below, as if this symbol for spirit (the bird) is reconnecting it to the earthly reality. The picture is painted as a stained glass window that is surrounded by brown vaults. This points to a religious dimension: the integration of the fourth, the divine aspect of the lower world, into the upper light of the Christian trinity, the yellow triangle.

BLACK

Black is the first non-colour which we are going to consider. It is experienced as darkness, where no sight and orientation is possible. Black therefore points to a loss of consciousness, death, chaos, fear, depression and, of course, also to the devil.

But out of the darkness there also comes the new light, which is why black is also the colour of resurrection and possible rejuvenation. The morning goddess Isis has a black coat, under which all the colours are hidden, pointing to the mystery of her ability to give birth to new life after death, out of her dark black womb. The black Madonna, found at so many places of pilgrimage such as Einsiedeln (Switzerland), Tschenstochau (Poland), Montserrat (Spain) points to the same mystery. In alchemy, the blackness (*nigredo*) is the necessary prerequisite for the whiteness (*albedo*) and the redness (*rubedo*), which means the resurrection of new life after the depressed state of the *nigredo*.

Materials like coal, lead, tar and pitch are black. It is the colour of Saturn, the god of bondage to earth, limitation and depression. We speak commonly of a black hole we can get into or of a black day when we have misfortune or are depressed.

But dirty black coal is also an important source of energy; heavy lead is also the origin of the gold of the sages in alchemy; tar and pitch are even symbols of the Stone of the Sages in Arabic alchemy. And the black hole of a depression can turn into a womb out of which the ego can be reborn and rejuvenated.

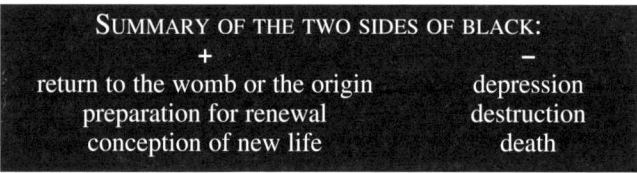

SUMMARY OF THE TWO SIDES OF BLACK:	
+	**−**
return to the womb or the origin	depression
preparation for renewal	destruction
conception of new life	death

The colour black can point to nature's destructive or regenerative side on a very basic level.

Colour Symbolism 105

Fig. 85: Picture by a 32-year-old woman (see also Fig. 139). She suffered from depression. Out of the blackness this picture emerged. It is a symbol of wholeness, a so-called mandala, that is connected to an inner dynamism: four enigmatic winged beings. A multicoloured ring is connected to the mandala. It looks like a handle for pulling it out from the womb of the black depths into consciousness. Indeed, this picture inspired further pondering and led to many further pictures (see also figures 69 (p. 91) and 124 (p. 145), painted by the same woman).

Fig. 86: Watercolour, painted by a 22-year-old man (see also figures 75 and 143). The black landscape with the cave reveals some insights. The man, who was suffering from a compulsive attachment to a woman, gets an insight from this picture into the «face» of his overwhelming daemonic fascination. It is all connected and surrounded by black lines, including the eye and even the pupil. It shows that out of all this blackness a light could finally come into the hand of the red man in the cave, a representation of the man who painted the picture.

Grey

Grey is also a non-colour, experienced in grey clouds and in fog, grey rocks and mountains, grey ashes, asphalt and the grey hair of ageing people.

Being the union of the most extreme opposites (black and white), grey is also an important «mediation colour». Like green and violet, grey is associated with the mediator god Mercury, whose metal is grey mercury. Grey emphasises the union of the most extreme opposites of life and death. In this way it also carries a mystical quality that can inspire humans. Thus, a misty grey day can enable human beings to feel the importance of a reflective disentanglement from «colourful» attachments.

But on the other hand, one speaks in general of grey nebulous times and of grey theories, to express a lack of emotional heights and depths, and of lifeless abstractions. This would point to the narrowing, life-absorbing quality of grey, where neither life nor death is really present, only an unhealthy, sad mixture of these opposites.

Summary of the two sides of Grey:	
+	–
union of extreme opposites	mixture of extreme opposites
possibility of abstraction	over-theoretical
detached holding back of colours	sad lack of colour
symbol of wisdom	symbol of deterioration

Grey can be understood as a symbol of wise detachment from life *or* a sad lack of life.

Fig. 87: Picture by a 28-year-old woman. The grey background of this picture in an expression of her «grey background-sadness». It is in strong contrast to the intensity of colours of the snake, which carries symbols of wholeness (See also Fig. 99, p. 125).

WHITE

White, when it absorbs all the colours of rays of light, paradoxically becomes a non-colour, like black and grey.

The colour white is basically associated—depending on the region of the world—with dead bodies, sun-dried bones in the desert, or snow and ice in colder regions. Therefore, white is commonly linked with purity, absence of feelings and emotions and with death. In China and India it is the colour of mourning.

By way of contrast, milk, the life-giving liquid; and salt, which gives flavour to food and is crucial to life, are also white. This provides a connection between white and life.

As white shows dirt easily, it is associated with purity and innocence. In German we have the expression «*eine weisse Weste haben*» (literal translation: to wear a clean vest), which means in English to have a clean record.

A white garment, devoid of any colour, can easily be dyed. *Candidus* in Latin means white, and that is where the word «candidate» comes from. For rites of passage—such as baptism, communion, marriage, death—white garments are often worn. Thus white symbolizes the willingness to be «dyed» again, meaning the willingness to adopt a new attitude.

Natural science tells us that white is either the sum of all colours or the absence of all colours.

SUMMARY OF THE TWO SIDES OF WHITE:	
+	**−**
life	death
transition to something new	departure from something
immortality	annihilation
light and purity	cold detachment

White can be understood as a life-giving basis of the unconscious or as the chilly absence of all life.

White space can point either to something that cannot be touched (for example a bewildering autonomous complex) or, on the other hand, to something like a «window to eternity» that opens and allows unexpected new aspects of life to enter (see, for instance, Fig. 105 on page 131).

e. Mixed Colours in General

Let us take an example: *dark blue,* as the colour of the night-sky or the night-water, lies between blue and black.

The symbolism of this mixed colour can be understood (as we have seen with green, orange and violet) by looking at the meaning of the colours involved in the mixture:

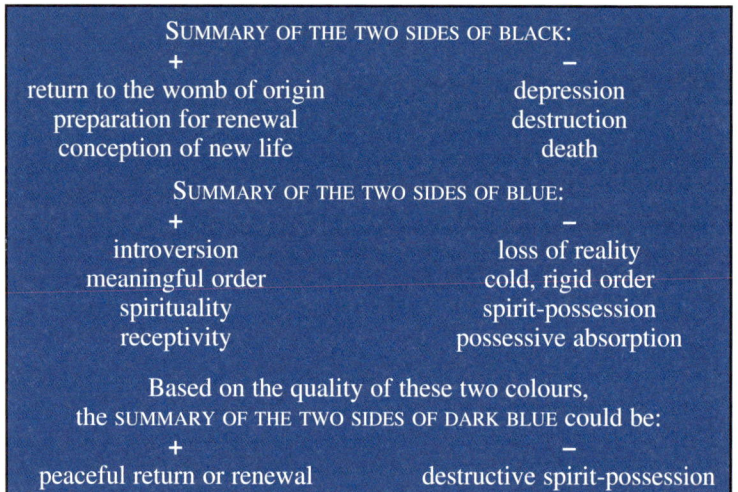

As we can see with dark blue, all the nuances of different mixtures of colours can be understood by the symbolism of the colours involved.

As the following example shows, the colour *pink* is a union of the vitalizing or destructive red and the life-giving or live-absorbing white.

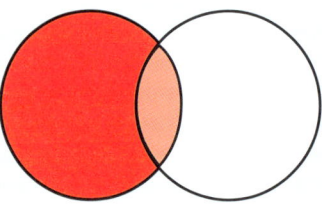

Psychologically this points on the one hand to the renewing *or* infantile «baby-pink». On the other hand pink can point to a red that is made light *or* is tempered by the non-colour white. The pink «Stone of the Sages» symbolizes the goal of the alchemical work: the union of the red male with the white feminine.

The main things to keep in mind are the two sides of each archetype, its constructive or destructive manifestation. Which aspect of the two sides has to be given preference in our interpretation depends on the context of the entire picture.

3.6. Number Symbolism

As number symbolism is rather difficult to understand and because of this is usually a neglected aspect in picture interpretation, this topic will be treated in greater detail.

a. The Symbolic Nature of Numbers

When talking about numbers, we usually think of them as quantities: numbers on coins and notes, house numbers, phone numbers, statistics, etc. This quantitative aspect of numbers helps us to orient ourselves in our civilised world. Yet in addition to the quantity aspect in numbers, each natural number also has a qualitative dimension that illuminates its unique and particular characteristics, or the peculiar flavour that belongs only to this or that specific number. For example, only the number two is related to polarity, as all pairs of opposites are made up of two parts: up and down, man and woman, right and wrong, left and right. And only the number four is connected with the quality of complete orientation, as seen, for instance, in the cross of the four directions: north, south, east and west. Looked at in this way, natural numbers become like individuals, each one different from the other, each one embodying its own unique essence: its own essential quality.[17]

This qualitative aspect of numbers has been extensively treated in the vast amount of literature on number symbolism, where the various cultures provide their associations. In exploring how the qualitative dimension of numbers is regarded in different cultures, we can find striking similarities.[18] These, however, can easily seduce us by misleading one-sided statements and oversimplifications by using pat formulas such as: «two is feminine», «three is masculine», «five is eros», «eleven and thirteen are unfavourable numbers», etc.[19] These one-sided statements with regard to the qualitative

---

[17] See M.-L. von Franz, *Number and Time*, p. 74f.
[18] See for instance F.C. Endres and A. Schimmel, *Mystery of Numbers*.
[19] This tendency can be found for instance in J. Jacobi's book, *Vom Bilderreich der Seele*. L. Paneth, in his book *Zahlensymbolik im Unbewusstsein*, also makes such absolute statements.

aspect of individual numbers do not take into account the fact that remarkable differences also exist in the way each number is characterised in different cultures. For instance, not all cultures have the same holy or unlucky numbers. And a number that is considered as male in one culture can be female in another.[20] Thus with regard to the qualitative aspect of numbers, it is important to keep in mind that when looking at different cultures, we find not only similarities but differences as well.

At first this might appear somewhat confusing, but we have to realise that numbers are not signs created by the conscious mind and representing a fixed meaning. Numbers are more than mere signs. They are—in the same way as our other criteria for understanding pictures—*symbols* arising from the unconscious psyche through the actualisation of an archetype.[21] This connection between number and archetype can, for instance, be seen in the religions of ancient Mesopotamia and of the Mayans.[22] In these religions, each natural number was either identical to or associated with a specific god. In these cultures, numbers were considered to be the manifestation of something transcendental and not just as man-made products.[23] As such, numbers acted in the manner of any symbol, leading consciousness into ever-deeper insights. This explains why absolute statements about natural numbers can only be half-truths, for they do not take into account the archetypal dimension, which can only be accurately described by careful amplification. Therefore when relating to numbers, we have to be willing to suspend our most natural propensity to formulate simple equations that limit or even kill off the symbolic aspect of numbers.

Looking back into the historical development of our human perception of the world, we will understand why today we no longer consider numbers as symbols, but as clearly defined signs for quantities. Originally humans experienced and understood their world predominantly in the categories of magic-causality. This means that an occurrence could be understood and explained not only by an outer cause, but also by the influence of a god, a demon or through witchcraft. The gradual development of occidental scientific thinking defined the idea of causality more and more clearly and rejected the magical ideas of the past. Along with this came an increasingly pure quantitative definition of number, while its qualitative aspect increasingly rejected. The qualitative aspect of numbers that enables us to read the symbolic patterns of a constellated situation—as is well known, for instance, from the *I Ching*[24] and from other divination

---

[20] See M.-L. von Franz, *Number and Time*, p. 31.
[21] Ibid., p. 74.
[22] See C. Butler, *Number Symbolism in Europe*. This book traces the history of numerological allegory and has an excellent primary source bibliography.
[23] See M.-L. von Franz, op. cit., p. 144.
[24] *I Ching, The Book of Changes*, R.Wilhelm (ed.).

practices—was no longer a matter of scientific investigation. The strict limitation of modern science to causality means it can no longer relate to and understand the phenomena of meaningful coincidences. For this reason, C.G. Jung has suggested the term «synchronicity», in order that certain aspects of reality not included in the causal description of nature can be interpreted as synchronistic events *without the necessity of regressing into an archaic form of magical-causal thinking*.[25]

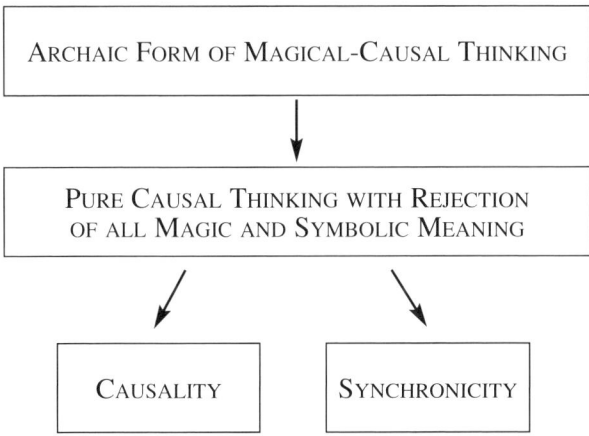

Fig. 88: The development of the archaic form of magical-causal thinking to the *complementarity of causality and synchronicity* (C.G. Jung).

The qualitative aspect of number therefore sank into the misty realm of esoteric speculations. When looking at books on number symbolism, we therefore often find a dubious mixture of solid matter-of-fact amplifications and magical-numerological speculations. In clear distinction to this sort of publication, Marie-Louise von Franz, in her book *Number and Time*, was able to show that the qualitative aspect of numbers can be distilled out of each number by collecting its characteristic manifestations from psyche and matter. By careful use of the method of amplification she was able to clarify the quality of the first four numbers. In this way, she

---

[25] See C.G. Jung and W. Pauli, *Naturerklärung und Psyche*. Jung's contribution, in English «Synchronicity, an acausal connecting principle», can be found in C.G. Jung, *Structure and Dynamics of the Psyche* [Coll. Works 8], § 816–968. These synchronistic events used to be a main focus for traditional Chinese thinking, which developed with the *I Ching* a numerical way of relating to the patterns constellated at a particular moment in time in regard to a particular question.

could complement the one-sided development of occidental scientific thinking with its purely quantitative understanding of number. Her careful procedure allows us to reintegrate the qualitative aspect of numbers into scientific thinking and thus to complement our mainly quantitative number concept *without falling back into magical-numerological speculations*.[26]

Using the method of amplification in the same way as in the previous chapters, we will see how each number appears—not only in nature but also in our unconscious psyche. However, before we embark on this, we need to explain the general function of numbers in the interpretation of pictures.

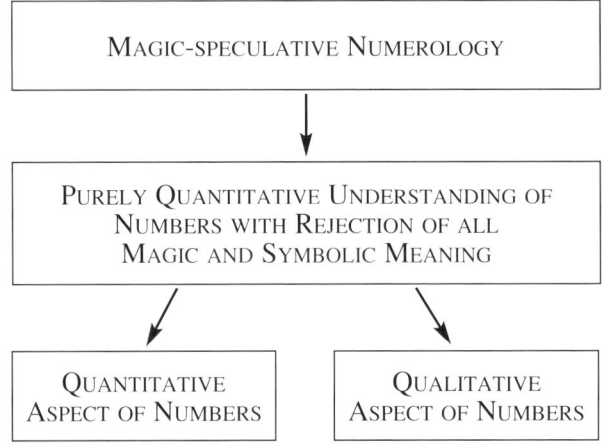

Fig. 89: The development from the archaic form of magic-speculative numerology to the *complementarity of the quantitative and the qualitative aspect of numbers* (Marie-Louise von Franz).

---

[26] See in detail in M.-L. von Franz, *Number and Time*, p. 85.

b. Numbers as Basic Elements of Order

Numbers bring order to consciousness.[27] For example, when one is volleying a badminton shuttlecock back and forth with a child, it is simple pleasure and amusement until the child decides to start keeping score. Then number introduces order, and there can be a winner and a loser. Whenever something is differentiated and therefore ordered, we can count the different parts through numbering. Because of this, numbers have been considered as the predestined instrument for creating order. But they are also an instrument for apprehending an already existing, but as yet unknown regular arrangement or orderedness.[28] Thus numbers can be considered as the most basic natural element of order and also as a basic tool to create a new order. Jung defined number as an *archetype of order which has become conscious*.[29] This would mean, as von Franz points out, that our idea of order has a preconscious aspect; it is based on an inborn disposition within our psyche.[30]

The basic connection between number and psyche becomes clearly visible when we consider the reflections of the zoologist B. Rentsch. He states that just as our bodies developed gradually out of inorganic matter, it is hardly likely that our psyche suddenly appeared in its fully evolved state. Furthermore, there is a mutual connection between psyche and body, as can be seen, for instance, in psychosomatic medicine. Rentsch points to the strong probability that even at the level of inorganic matter, the first psychic elements must have already existed side by side with matter.[31] In modern physics[32] and modern psychology[33], we find evidence that matter has an inherent proto-psyche that stood at the beginning of evolution and is characterised as psychic qualities of the structured matter that builds up our world. As matter without number is just an «undefined soup», this proto-psyche must be number-like.[34] Therefore, we may assume that the basic order of our psyche is number, which is, as Jung pointed out, *the most primitive manifestation of spirit.*[35]

---

[27] See M.-L. von Franz, *Number and Time*, p. 143.
[28] Ibid., p. 45.
[29] See C.G. Jung, *Structure and Dynamics of the Psyche* [Coll. Works 8], § 255–93.
[30] See M.-L. von Franz, op. cit., p. 143.
[31] See B. Rentsch, *Neuere Probleme der Abstammungslehre*. See also the commentary of C.G. Jung on «The Secret of the Golden Flower», *Alchemical Studies* [Coll. Works 13], § 34.
[32] See W. Pauli and C.G. Jung, *Atom and Archetype—the Pauli/Jung letters, 1932–1958*.
[33] Mainly the discovery of the psychoid aspect of the archetype by C.G. Jung, *On the Nature of Psyche*, [Coll. Works 8], § 368–86.
[34] Personal communication with Dr von Franz.
[35] C.G. Jung, *Synchronicity: An Acausal Connecting Principle*, [Coll. Works 8], § 870 and C.G. Jung, *The Archetypes and the Collective Unconscious*, [Coll. Works 9,1], § 393.

As is well known from physics, numbers make visible the quality of different processes of transformation in matter. One example of this is the change of quality in an atom when adding a particle. In a similar way, numbers also play a key-role in the arrangement of psychic order and in the process of psychic transformation, as we will see later, for instance, in the development of consciousness. As numbers are obviously at the basis of order, both in matter and in the psyche, they appear to be the mysterious *common language of all creation, particularly in its aspect of meaning*.[36]

On the basis of these general points regarding the influence of numbers in matter and in our psychic structure, we can reflect upon the importance of number symbolism in understanding pictures. For in the same way as the number of particles determines the quality of the atom, the number of elements in a picture qualifies in a specific way this particular element. It reveals which aspect of the archetype of order was at that time constellated, be it in connection with a particular motif or be it with regard to the picture as a whole.

Fig. 90: Drawn by a 38-year-old man.

---

[36] Different divination methods, especially the *I Ching*, are based on numbers, because they are the bridge to «pure nature», beyond consciousness, See more in M.-L. von Franz, *Number and Time,* p. 284 and M.-L. von Franz, *On Divination and Synchronicity.*

Let us take as an example a picture (see Fig. 90), drawn spontaneously by a 38-year-old man who suffered from a typical midlife crisis. In his despair he wanted to show me how he felt at that time—he wanted to bring me «into the picture» of his actual situation. The author painted himself, suspended on a rope, close to the centre of the picture. We see how desperate he must have felt in his situation.

We see here *two* suns. This gives the picture a quite different quality compared with what there would have been with just one sun. The sun as a symbol of consciousness that appears doubled can be understood as a split in consciousness. This would mean that at that time the author of the picture could not bring the two represented worlds together. He was expressing his suspension in a split value system. On the left side are the values of nature and a grounded traditional, but at the same time not very exciting, married life. The box on the left side is an oscillograph that shows no activity or excitement. On the right side of the picture, we see a similar oscillograph, showing great excitement: the attraction of modern town life with its freedom. The sports car and the woman's face behind the city skyline symbolise the fascination with this other world with its speed and its convenient lack of commitment. The author of the picture—by profession a quite successful manager—could not reconcile these two worlds: a well-grounded life with the values of his Christian tradition on the one hand and the exciting seductive freedom of the modern world on the other hand. At the time of painting this picture, he fell in love with a woman other than his wife—not exactly a rare occurrence around the time of the «midday of life». This painful suspension in the two-ness of his psychic state forced him to go into himself and find out about the meaning of this fateful split.

After this general introduction to the quality aspect of numbers, we will now work on understanding the symbolism of the numbers 1 to 17 by amplifying each individual number. We will not go beyond the number 17, since in pictures we rarely find such great numbers.

c. Amplification of the First Ten Numbers

For the amplification of the different numbers we will examine how humans experienced these numbers in daily life. These observations will be accompanied by significant statements which emerge from the observation of numbers in matter. Sometimes we will also make a reference to how a particular number is seen in mythology. But it is not our aim to get an overview for each number in the mythology of different cultures. For this I must refer to existing encyclopaedias on number symbolism. The chosen material is intended simply to give some major characteristics for each number (see Fig. 92) in so far as it becomes relevant to the understanding of pictures.

NUMBER 1

As the first number of the infinite series of natural numbers, the number 1 stands before the beginning of all ordering or, in other words, before the creative process begins. At the same time, the one also comes at the end of a creative process, uniting the different parts again. In matter, a series of atoms makes one molecule; a series of molecules makes one cell; a series of cells makes one organism, etc.

As quantity, the one stands not only at the beginning of all natural numbers, but it is also connected to all the other numbers. This is because by adding «another one», we come to the next natural number. By this process we arrive at an infinite row of natural numbers, which corresponds—as Jung once pointed out—to the uncountable number of individual creatures.[37] As the one is connected with the infinite row of natural numbers it leads to infinity. An image can illustrate this quantitative aspect of the one.

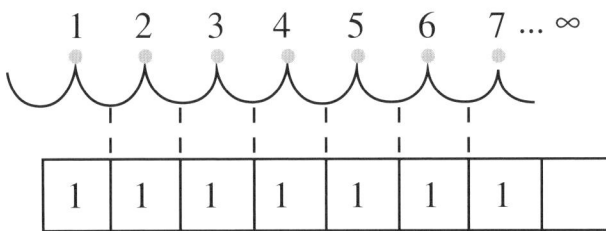

Fig. 91: The number 1 as individual number and basis of all natural numbers. Above, the one is at the beginning, *one among many yet at the same time the unique*.[38] Below, the number 1 forms the unit by which every number is born out of the previous one, the *one being the basic rhythm* (see also Fig. 92).

---

[37] C.G. Jung, *Memories, Dreams, Reflections*, p. 287.

[38] Different from all other numbers, the one does not, for instance, multiply by itself or reduce itself by division, because it is the divisor of all the other numbers (see M.-L. von Franz, *Number and Time*, p. 61ff).

Number Symbolism 117

Besides this quantitative aspect of each number, considered in terms of the one, we look at numbers in terms of qualities. This means that, for instance, the number 2 is not only a halved or doubled «original number one» but also the symmetry aspect of the original number one (see Fig. 92). On this basis, von Franz suggests that we talk of a «*one-continuum*», which goes on into the two. In other words, the two is somehow already immanent in the original one. It is «a specific quality of the one-continuum at a given time».[39] Likewise, in the «two-aspect» of the one, the three is immanent as the synthesis or as the symmetrical axis in the bipolarity of the one-continuum.[40]

Marie-Louise von Franz talks of numbers as a time-bound quality

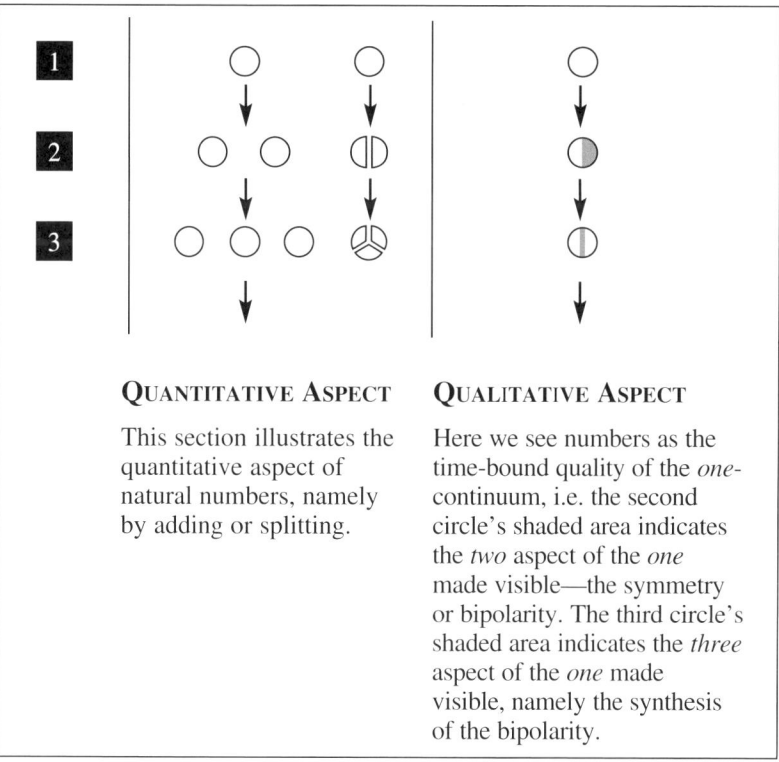

QUANTITATIVE ASPECT

This section illustrates the quantitative aspect of natural numbers, namely by adding or splitting.

QUALITATIVE ASPECT

Here we see numbers as the time-bound quality of the *one-continuum*, i.e. the second circle's shaded area indicates the *two* aspect of the *one* made visible—the symmetry or bipolarity. The third circle's shaded area indicates the *three* aspect of the *one* made visible, namely the synthesis of the bipolarity.

Fig. 92: The quantitative and the qualitative aspect of the natural numbers.[41]

---

[39] See M.-L. von Franz, *Number and Time*, p. 63.
[40] Ibid, p. 64 and 75.
[41] I owe this overview to a conversation with Dr Marie-Louise von Franz.

of the one-continuum. They signify different rhythmic configurations of the one-continuum.[42] This means that at different moments in time, different numbers are the best possible explanation for the quality of the situation. For instance, in moments of deep ambivalence, two is the best possible expression for that state of being, as we have seen in the picture by the 38-year-old manager (Fig. 90 on p. 114). Out of that situation a solution may be born that would lead to a new flow of life, best symbolised by the three. Numbers signify different rhythmic configurations of the one-continuum. In this way, the one contains qualitatively the whole sequence of natural numbers.

From this we can summarise by saying that the one is a symbol for the still undivided wholeness, the origin. As result of a creative process, the one also stands for the goal, the end; and for individuation, which means the creative process of an individual realising more and more his or her inner unity and unique being. As unity, the number one symbolises the final union of everything and in this way the all-uniting supreme godhead. Since the number one is linked to all natural numbers, the one unites the paradox of uniqueness and of being one among many.

The one characterises a psychological attitude where a human life is still in archaic identity with its surroundings, in «*participation mystique*», or on a conscious level, where a human feels at one with creation.

In the picture below (Fig. 93), we see this oneness with creation as represented in a painting by Japanese artist, Y. Awakawa, with an accompanying verse by Serg-ts'an Suzuki.[43]

If one thing is dominating a picture, this can point either to a unity

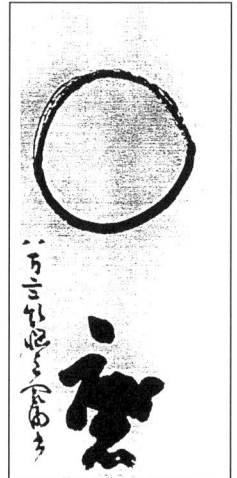

One in all
All in one—
If only this is realized
No more worry about your not being perfect

The believing mind is not divided
And undivided is the believing mind
This is where words fail
For it is not of the past, future, or present.

Fig. 93:
Japanese ink-painting by
Y. Awakawa.

---

[42] See M.-L. von Franz, *Number and Time*, Chapter 4.
[43] See M.-L. von Franz, *Time, Rhythm, and Response*, p. 63.

Number Symbolism 119

that is still unconscious *or* to a union on a higher level. The following picture illustrates such a state of a hardly differentiated single motif.

On a sheet of newspaper a 51-year-old unmarried woman did a

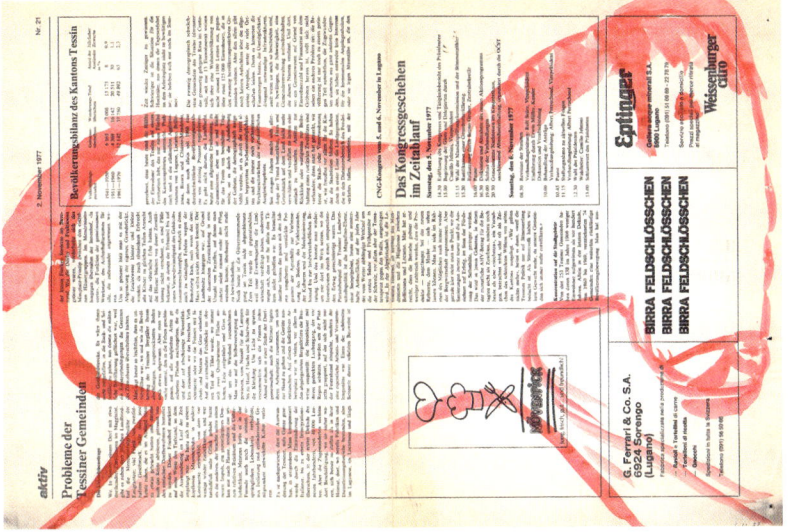

Fig. 94: Drawn by a 51-year-old woman.

drawing at the beginning of her analysis (see Fig. 94). She was suffering from an unresolvable love problem. The animal, painted in red watercolour, she called a horse. Her image is an expression of a still completely archaic, unreflected view of an aspect of her animal side. Psychologically it mirrors a coming to view of something central that is emerging from the collective «newspaper-background». It is a symbolic expression of her unfulfilled strong erotic longing. But at the same time, this horse also points to the emerging of a rough contour of a strong helpful animal (horsepower!) which, as it later turned out, carried her through a long and in-depth analysis to a completely new view of her love problem. In this way she was able to realise that her bodily urges led her to become aware of being unique and a unity on a more conscious level.

Whenever a fantasy, depression or some other problem is overwhelming, «this single issue» is painted first. For instance, everything is painted black at the beginning. Often, in a second or later picture, a differentiation takes place. For instance, a spot may be painted on the otherwise totally black painted sheet. With the appearance of a division, *«Auseinandersetzung»* (a form of inner debate) becomes possible, and with this we come to the number two.

NUMBER 2

With the number 2 the quality of symmetry, polarity and discrimination comes up. The «two-aspect of the one» has, therefore, to do with concrete creation, the reality we live in. We all experience life in duality, in polar tension. The wholeness of existence consists of life and death, waking and sleeping, active and passive, male and female or —as the Chinese name it—yang and yin.

A common experience of the «two-aspect» of life is, for example, the waking-up experience. Out of sleep, we wake up to the realisation: «I exist». There is a world and here I am. There is an object and here is a subject. In a comparable way, the original unity and participation of early childhood is followed by a waking-up, and a sense of being different from one's surroundings and an awareness of gender and of good and evil. That is also the reason why the number two in Christianity has been associated with the devil and a feminine, since both «Lucifer» (Latin = light-bringer) and Eve brought opposition to the one God, leading to exile from the original paradise—out into the hardships of everyday life. Along with the two comes doubt (from Latin *dubius* = dual), splits, opposites and quarrels, as the two poles have to remain apart by tension in order not to merge back again into the one.

In dreams we observe that motifs of two identical things have to do with *border (or liminal) phenomena*. These are contents which have just arrived at the border between consciousness and the unconscious.[44] «When a content comes up and touches the threshold of consciousness, it is cut into two parts, into a one and the other. The one is the aspect that I can state, while the other remains in the unconscious.»[45] The relation of the number two with phenomena at the fringe of consciousness also becomes visible in the fact that in nearly all cultures and religions of the world, two identical demons or divine figures represent the symbolic guardians of the entrance to the beyond.[46]

In order to become conscious of something, we have to discriminate, to «cut apart». This is why a content which appears at the fringe of consciousness is immediately cut apart by the light of discrimination. The devil is named *diabolos* in Greek, which comes from the Greek verb *diaballein* (= to throw apart). Therefore the number two has to do with the development of consciousness, which in Christian tradition, became linked with sin and evil. When something is reflected—for instance in the mirror of still, clear water—it also appears doubled: the original and the mirror-image. This doubling by reflection is also associated with the development of

---

[44] See C.G. Jung, *Seminar über Kinderträume*, p. 72.
[45] See M.-L. von Franz, *Individuation in Fairytales*, p. 27.
[46] See M.-L. von Franz, *Number and Time*, p. 92.

Number Symbolism 121

consciousness, as is illustrated in the famous myth of Narcissus and Echo.[47] If we look at the outer physical aspects of our «fringe of consciousness», we find quite concretely the dominance of the number two: two eyes, two ears, two nostrils and, of course, two hands and two feet. And in connection with the development of human consciousness, we see that it is based on the cerebrum with its two lobes.

Psychologically a dualistic world and image of God symbolises tension, doubt and criticism of everything: of God, life, nature and oneself.[48] The dominance of the number two in a picture therefore points to a basic «not being at one with oneself». Whether this is a pathological situation, or rather points to the coming realisation of a new consciousness, depends upon the context of the picture. The oscillating «yes and no», «up and down», «back and forth» is often seen in the meandering lines of schizophrenic or seriously neurotic people. We often find this expressed in oscillating motives or lines such as in the following picture that is taken from Hans Prinzhorn's classic book about pictures of mentally ill people.[49] It is a continuation and perpetuation of an up and down, and up and down.

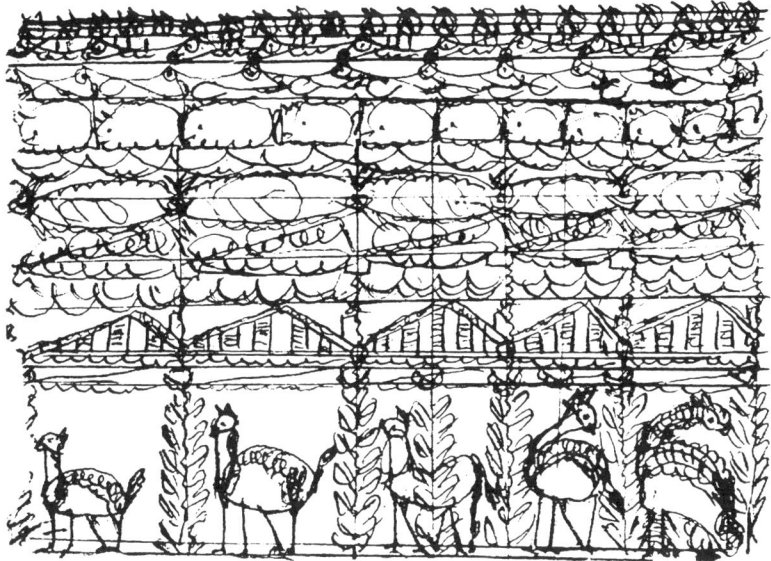

Fig. 95: Picture, drawn on toilet paper by a patient who suffered from schizophrenia.[50]

---

[47] Ovid, *Metamorphosis,* Book III, 339–510.
[48] See M.-L. von Franz, *Number and Time,* Chapter 5.
[49] H. Prinzhorn, *Bildnerei der Geisteskranken.* Ibid., p. 68.
[50] See M.-L. von Franz, *Number and Time,* p. 103.

In figure 90, we could also see a clear two-ness, a split into two halves. But instead of a pathological rupture, it shows rather a painful ambivalence (*ambo* in Latin means both), in which the author is suspended. In the following picture (Fig. 96) by a 27-year-old woman, we find a dominance of static polarities or symmetries.

Fig. 96: Painted by a 27-year-old woman (see also Fig. 72, 73, 84).

In addition to the strong emphasis of the number two we also find a uniting third: the yellow globe with the inserted moon form. This «uniting third» motif points to the idea that consciousness (yellow) could be born out of the experience of the opposites. And, indeed, something new could be born out of the realisation of her spiritual life (bird motif), which was at that time completely flat and fixed in different opinions. With this we now come to the number three.

Number Symbolism

NUMBER 3

In contrast to the basic experience of the two as division or as the eternal oscillatory rhythm of «night and day», «life and death», or «yang and yin», the number 3 introduces a directional element.[51] If we look, for instance, at an individual living creature, we find that in addition to its being bound to the steady «rhythm of the two»—for example waking and sleeping, taking and giving—there is also a change or development taking place. The three stands for this irreversible process in time.[52] Time is experienced in past, present and future. And since in the whole of creation, there is both a causal and a final development line to be observed, namely the evolutionary process, the number three becomes connected to this inner determination. This dynamism has been understood as fate. In mythological products of the unconscious psyche, fate divinities—for instance the Fates, Norns or the Parsee—usually appear in triadic form.

Taken as the union of opposites, the three appears as the new creation, the child. Three is the result of the tension and the attraction of the opposites and relates psychologically to the birth of consciousness.[53] Consciousness is the third that comes in addition to the eternal rhythm of the opposites. Consciousness is the awareness of the one creation that manifests itself in infinite polarities. The three therefore deals with actualising the «two-aspect of the one» in time and space: on the one side in human consciousness and on the other side in creation.[54]

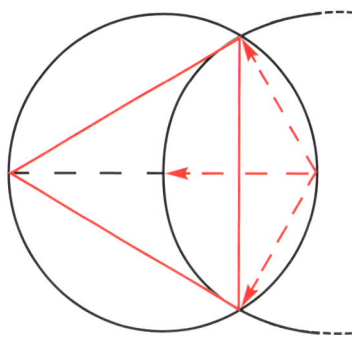

Fig. 97: The number 3 and its relation to cyclical time. The radius divides the circle in a way that allows us to draw an isosceles triangle.

---

[51] Balzac says: "Three is the formula of all creation" (from R. Allendy, *Le symbolisme des nombres*, p. 42).

[52] The number three is therefore qualitatively connected to the change at the basis of the oscillating rhythm in creation. The *I Ching* (Book of Changes) builds the bridge to this beyond with two trigrams. For this and for the relation of the three to the genetic code, see M.-L. von Franz, *Number and Time*, p. 105f.

[53] The word *Gnosis* is related to the Greek work *gignomai* = to be born.

[54] See M.-L. von Franz, *Number and Time*, p. 109.

The appearance of the number three in a picture can thus indicate the beginning of a development towards a personal standpoint, towards ego-consciousness. Yet any synthesis in nature is only for a given moment a resolving of the tension between opposites. This also holds true in the psychic realm. A new insight or the birth of a numinous new symbol[55] is never an absolute truth, although, once we have it, we tend again and again to cling to such a conscious standpoint or numinous experience. That is the reason why Jung pointed out, in his paper on the Trinity, that we must consider the three only as a *relative wholeness*.[56]

It seems to be in connection with the Christian identification of the Trinity with one side of reality, namely the masculine side, that absolute statements about the number three go in this direction. Freud, for instance, regarded the three as typically masculine, as he saw the phallic form in the triangle.[57] Yet the delta or the triangle was already used in Neolithic portrayals of women to represent their genitals. The Indian *yoni* is also represented by a triangle. And, in the Western tradition, the down-pointing triangle was the sign of the feminine water while the up-pointing triangle was the sign of the masculine fire (see Fig. 98).

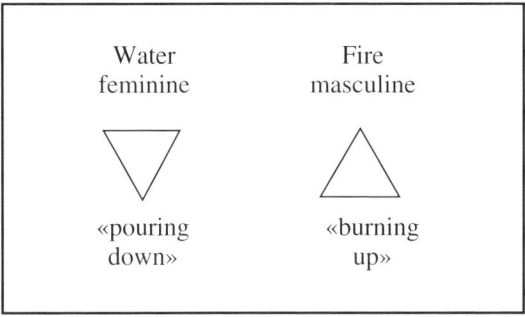

Fig. 98: The two aspects of the triangle.

From this we can again see that *we just cannot make any simple equations* when trying to understand the quality aspect of numbers.

---

[55] The word *symbolon* is related to the Greek *symballein* = to throw together (and we had, with the number two, the word *diaballein* = to throw apart).

[56] C.G. Jung, *Psychology and Religion, West and East* [Coll. Works 11], §§ 169–295, see also M.-L. von Franz, *Number and Time*, p. 124ff.

[57] See F.C. Endres and A. Schimmel, *The Mystery of Numbers,* p. 88.

Whenever the number three appears in a dream or a picture, we can assume that whatever is connected to this number is now actively influencing or possessing the ego. In the following picture (Fig. 99) by a 28-year-old woman, we see, for instance, three black arms that keep a wonderfully coloured snake up in the air. The snake, which normally lives on the ground, is held away from the ground by three arms of unseen figures. The fateful aspect of their action is symbolised by the fact that the arms are

Fig. 99: Drawn by a 28-year-old woman.

three in number. The snake consists mainly of a backbone and is thus a symbol of the knowledge of our unconscious reptilian background, which manifests itself in the reactions of our vegetative nervous system, centred around our backbone. Psychologically, the snake symbolises the reactions of our unconscious, like autonomous body reactions, dreams, visions and fantasies. That is why the snake is also connected in many cultures with the healing wisdom of nature, which, however, has to be recognised and respected. The picture gives an image of what is going on behind the woman's back. Her «snake-soul» is not allowed to touch the ground and live in reality. We are «put in the picture» about why she was suffering from a depressive feeling of being cut off from the intensity of real life and its meaning. A fourth element, a green hand, tries to bring the head and the tail of the snake together in an attempt to unite the "upper" and the "lower" spheres, turning the snake into the famous ouroborus—the tailbiter. This symbolic unification, however, is achieved rather by grace than by force (see also Fig. 96 by the same woman).

On the other hand, the number three can also point to the beginning of a fateful new development. The following picture (Fig. 100) by a 24-year-old man came at the beginning of analysis and, with the dominance of the number three, shows that the motifs represented are going to demand careful attention.

Fig. 100: Painted by a 24-year-old man.

The rose, the aroused cobra, and the magician's wand have to be seen and properly taken into account. It is a triad of symbols that belongs to the realm of the earth goddess, a realm that the Christian value-system of the painter rather despised: 1. the red rose of the goddess of love; 2. the earth-bound cobra with its venom, and 3. the outer-rational realm of magic, which used to be mainly «the science of the feminine goddesses» (e.g. Isis). The appearance of such a picture at the beginning of analysis sets the task clearly. It means a fateful constellation (three objects) of his rejected and bewitched dark side of the feminine that wants and has to be looked at and, in time, properly understood and hence redeemed.

Number 4

Four is the first non-prime numeral of the natural numbers. It can be divided by two, or—in other words—it is made up of two times two or two plus two. This brings into focus the first basic quality of the number 4. The «four-aspect of the one» is the manifestation of the symmetry «within the symmetry of the one-continuum».

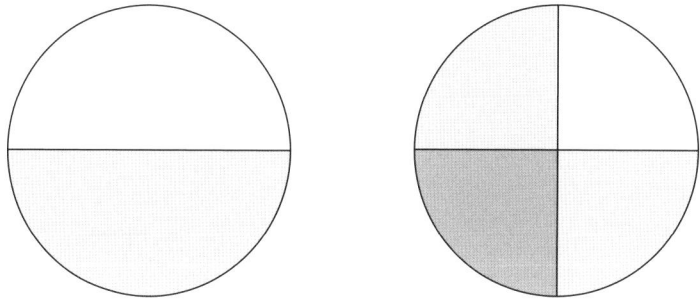

Fig. 101: The «four-aspect of the one».

If we take, for instance, a day as a unit, there is both the night aspect and the daylight aspect to it. The two aspects again have an inner symmetry: morning and afternoon on the one hand, and before midnight and after midnight on the other. The same model is also applied to get a complete orientation of units in a moon's complete cycle, namely the month. The four phases found their way into the sub-unit of the week. Four weeks make a full cycle from one full moon to the next. And four seasons make the full cycle of the year. With a four-fold structure we get an optimum of orientation, namely the four directions of the compass, the four elements, and the four human temperaments or the Cartesian cross in mathematics. All over the world we find the four-fold structure, with which humanity has attempted to establish a complete orientation.⁵⁸ This four-fold structure is immanent in our basic visual apperception. We have two eyes. They lie on a horizontal line. Since the two eyes see three-dimensionally, a vertical central line is implied between them. By these two lines, the vertical and horizontal one, the orientation cross of our view is unconsciously always present (see Fig. 102)

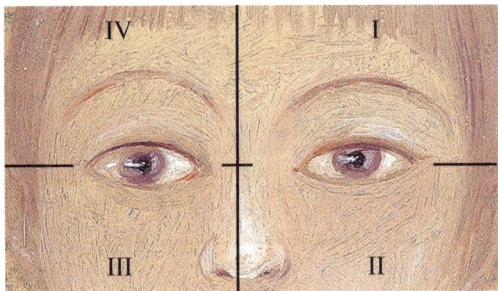

Fig. 102: The orientation cross of human vision is based on the structure of our eyes. It is unconsciously always present.

As we saw earlier, there are four functions at the disposal of consciousness. Through the act of becoming conscious, the four basic aspects of experiencing a content are rendered visible.⁵⁹

In her book *Number and Time*, M.-L. von Franz gives various examples of how the number four is connected to the transmission of information (in DNA, RNA, etc.).⁶⁰ On the basis of this and the previous observations, we can say that the number four is qualitatively connected to *complete conscious orientation*.

With the number four we reach a definite limit beyond which something new begins.⁶¹ As an illustration of this border, we have the German saying that somebody is the «fifth wheel on a car», meaning, that if somebody joins four people this person is superfluous. Mathematically speaking, the sum of the first four numbers (1 + 2 + 3 + 4) is ten, the limit of our counting with ten fingers. The three dimensions of space, together with time as the fourth, or the three aspects of time (past, present and future), together with space as the fourth, provide the frame of our conscious existence.⁶² The four-fold structure can also be connected to the two-times-two

---

[58]   See M.-L. von Franz, *Number and Time*, p. 115.
[59]   See C.G. Jung, *Psychological Types* [Coll. Works 6], § 556ff.
[60]   See M.-L. von Franz. *Number and Time*, p. 116f.
[61]   Ibid., p. 114f.

Number Symbolism

extremities on which most warm-blooded animals stand, and out of which the human species developed. Many cultural forms are consequently based on this model as well: four legs for beds, tables, chairs; four walls for our rooms and houses in most parts of the world; four wheels on our cars; four corners of our fields and so on.

From all this we can see that the number four is the archetypal background by which ego-consciousness is structured. Jung called this basis of consciousness the Self. Whenever the «four-aspect of the one» is constellated in a picture or in a motif, we can therefore assume that this particular content is being objectively recognised and is not, as we saw with the number three, actively influencing or possessing the ego. This means that four-fold structures form the unconscious connection to the activation of the archetype of the Self.[63] According to the context, the number four can then either point to a need for a union of divergent opposites by the act of becoming conscious *or* it can point to the realisation of the inborn unity of the opposites.

I remember a picture brought by a young man who had just painted a blue cross on a chaotic red background. He was in a state of great emotional upheaval and felt relieved and much calmer after painting this. In our context, the four-fold sign of the cross could be understood as a symbol of orientation. It gave him, for the time being, a feeling of order with regard to an overwhelming emotion.

The cross used to be—not only in Christian tradition—a well-known symbol in order to establish or to maintain order, in the way we still do in science with the Cartesian cross. The Cartesian cross is the modern way of establishing an order or structuring a complex situation (see Fig. 103).

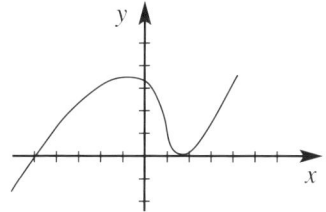

Fig. 103: Cartesian cross

---

[62] See C.G. Jung, *Aion* [Coll. Works 9/II], § 395–398.
[63] Ibid., Chapter 14.

130   Number Symbolism

In our next picture (Fig. 104), painted by a 39-year-old man, the four quarters point to the necessity or possibility of becoming conscious of a conflicting «compartment psychology». By this we mean that the four different parts are characterised by separation instead of cooperation. This unredeemed situation is the «cross» of the painter of this picture. The four basic colours, however, already connect the compartments.

Fig. 104: Painted by a 39-year-old man (see also Fig. 34, 37, 52, 53).

By way of contrast to figure 104, the next picture (Fig. 105) was painted by the same man two years later. It shows a first harmony of the four-fold structure. These opposites are symbolised by the four elements of earth, fire-sun (left), moon-water (right) and air on top. These four elements can work together in the living tree in its cyclical aspect of blossoming, fruit-bearing and wilting. This is a mirror of a new consciousness that could become aware of the basic unity of the opposites. But this experience of wholeness and peace is not yet protected against outer influences.

Fig. 105: Painted by a 41-year-old man.

NUMBER 5

The most common experience of the number 5 lies in examining one's own hand. The five fingers were the first tools enabling human beings to count. The word *digital* originates in the Latin word *digitus* = finger. The result of this counting with the help of the fingers was that the five, like the ten, became a natural counting limit. Roman numbers show this: We count I then II, III IIII or IV and for five we use a new sign V. Then we add to the V again single lines like VI, VII etc. till the new sign X (ten) and after X we start anew again. In Greek, the word *penta* = five is related to *pan* = all. The five is not only related to our hand, but also to our human body (see Fig. 106).[64]

We have five extremities (head, two arms and two legs), five sense organs and, somewhat surprisingly, five quite well-defined reflex zones on each half of the body, upon which the well-known foot-reflex zone therapy is based.[65] This direct relation of the five to the human body helps us to understand why this number is so often symbolically connected to natural

---

[64] Agrippa of Nettesheim, *Liber quartus de occulta philosophia*.
[65] See H. Marquardt, *Reflexzonenarbeit am Fuss*.

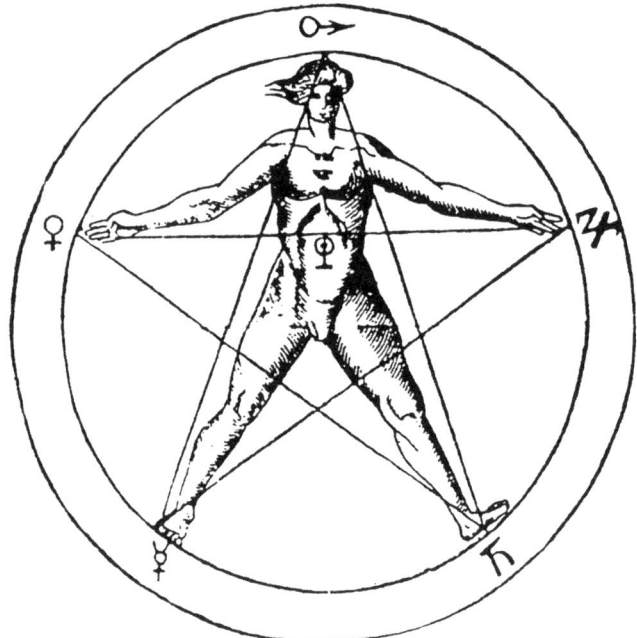

Fig. 106: Pentagram after Agrippa of Nettesheim.

man and to the microcosm, since human beings used to be looked upon as being a small cosmos. In Christianity, the five therefore became associated with everything corporeal and thus especially with lust, drives and sin.

Looked at mathematically, the five is a prime number. We arrive at five either by adding 4 + 1 or 3 + 2. As sum of 4 + 1, the five used to be considered that «special something» which goes beyond the four elements and gives life to organic matter.[66] This is why R. Allendy, in his book on number symbolism, states that the number five is the number of life.[67]

In inorganic structures, the regular pentagon practically does not exist.[68] It appears first in organic structures, such as the Rosaceae family in botany. The rose blossom, the flower of the apple tree and of the grapes happen to have a five-petalled structure.

---

[66] For details about the mathematical border between the number four and five see, A. Müller, *Einiges zur Symmetrie und Symbolik der Zahl Fünf*, p. 286.

[67] R. Allendy, *Le symbolisme des nombres*.

[68] See in detail K.A. Müller, *Einiges zur Symmetrie und Symbolik der Zahl Fünf*, pp. 283–285.

Number Symbolism 133

Fig. 107: Five as five petals.

As 2 + 3, the five is the union of the steady oscillating rhythm (number 2) and the dynamism of the process in time (number 3).[69]

If we look further at the quality of the «five-aspect of the one», this unifying quality becomes even more clearly visible, because with the five, as the middle of the cross of the doubled symmetry, the union of the two pairs of opposites is activated.

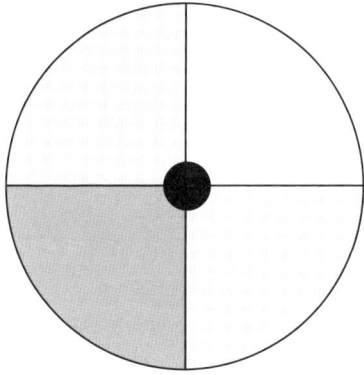

Fig. 108: The «five-aspect of the one-continuum».

---

[69] The Chinese connected the number 2 to earth and 3 to heaven. Thus five represents for them the union of earth and heaven.

The alchemical quintessence, as von Franz points out, does not additionally join onto the four as a fifth element, but rather, five represents the most spiritual and refined unity imaginable among the four elements. It is either initially present in them and is refined from them, or it is produced by the circulation of the one through the four elements.

The pentagon, with its five angles, geometrises the number five in its quantitative and additive form while the quintessence is represented by the quincunx as the centre of four.⁷⁰

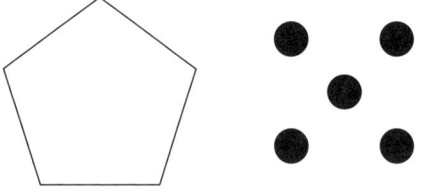

Fig. 109: The pentagon and the quincunx.

This quality of the quincunx as a mediator between the two pairs of opposites gives the number five a specific erotic dimension, as it is by «loving attraction» that opposites join together, as the old masters of alchemy described that unifying quality.⁷¹ This aspect of the five also becomes visible in the fact that the five is often connected to the love goddess, such as the Babylonian Ishtar or the Roman Venus, especially in the five-petal star of the pentagram, which in Christianity later came to be considered as a symbol in witchcraft (see Fig. 110).

Fig. 110: The pentagram became a symbol of devilish magic.⁷²

---

⁷⁰   M.-L. von Franz, *Number and Time*, p. 120f.
⁷¹   This is the main feature of the Stone of the Sages; the stone is the *quinta essentia* of the four elements. «He makes friends out of enemies.» See C.G. Jung, *Psychology and Alchemy* [Coll. Works 12].
⁷²   From R. Allendy, *Le symbolisme des nombres*, p. 139.

Martin Knapp, in his book *Pentagramma Veneris,* showed that the number five is surprisingly connected to the course of the planet Venus (see Fig. 111).[73] The quality of the number five is here mirrored in that aspect of nature.

Fig. 111: The course of the planet Venus around the sun is connected to the number five.

If the number five appears in a picture as five times the same motif or as five corners of a form, etc., we can assume that in regard to that motif *the possibility or necessity of relationship and its realization in life is activated.*

The following picture (Fig. 112) shows beautifully the symbolism of the five as the quintessence, which is born out of the loving relationship of the 34-year-old woman with a man, symbolized in the 2 x 2 hands. As *quinta essentia* the fifth here is the diamond, a well-known symbol in alchemy for the incorruptible diamond body or subtle body, which stands for the consolidated unique centre in the psyche of the individual.

---

[73] M. Knapp, *Pentagramma Veneris.* The 5th house in astrology is the house of eros.

Fig. 112: Painted by a 34-year-old woman.

In our next picture (Fig. 113), five men are trying in different ways to get the woman in the centre of the picture to stay down on earth and not to disappear with the white man into the blue beyond. The five men stand for the concrete relationship to life in this world. It is the five of earthly love that wants to get the 21-year-old female painter of this picture involved in real life. They try to get her back to the ground and not let her escape with her strong fantasy—symbolised by the long hair—to follow a white-painted «ghostly lover». On the other hand, we can see from the picture that the woman could maintain a loving relationship to «the man in the beyond», since he leaves five-petalled red «flower footprints», while she offers him a white flower. There are six of these red-coloured flowers, which brings us to the question of what the number six symbolizes.

Fig. 113: Painted by a 21-year-old woman (see also Fig. 140 on p. 159).

NUMBER 6

The number 6 is a so-called perfect number, because adding up as well as multiplying its divisors results in the number itself:

$$1 + 2 + 3 = 6$$
$$1 \times 2 \times 3 = 6$$

Taken as a sum, the six was looked upon as the union of the 3 and the 2 (in ancient China they represented heaven and earth) together with the original one (representing the creative principle). As such, the six stands for the completion or the union of creation and the creator.

Taken as the sum of 5 + 1, the six was also considered as the union of the natural man with the original number one, with his creator, the godhead. As 1 x 2 x 3, the six was understood as being composed of two triangles, joined in the one, (▽ + △ = ✡).

In medieval alchemical symbolism this sign represented the mysterious union of fire and water. This connection of the number six to the conjunction of the opposites can also be seen from the etymological relationship of six and «sex». The uniting centre as the sixth in the human representation within the pentagram is the sexual organ (see Fig. 114).

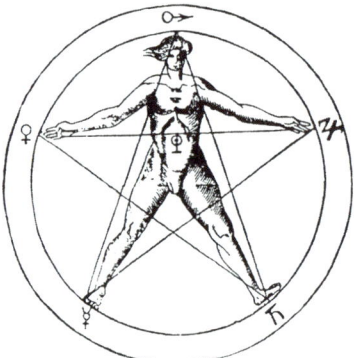
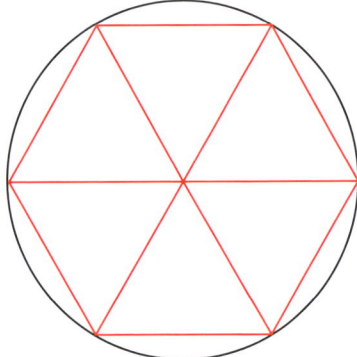

Fig. 114: Pentagram after Agrippa of Nettesheim.

Fig. 115: The circle can be divided by its radius into six equal parts.

Geometrically the six is connected to the perfect form, since a circle can be divided by its radius into six parts. The circle is the perfect form and a well-known symbol for totality and the godhead. Thus the hexagon is structured by the length of the radius, by God's measure, so to speak. Therefore, the number six is related to the whole of creation, the macrocosm and its creator.

Number Symbolism

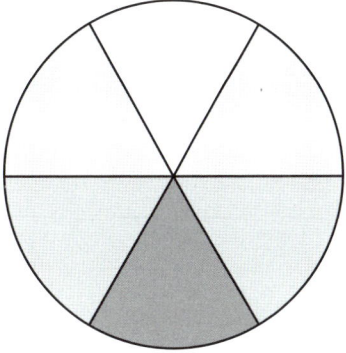

Fig. 116: The dividing up of the circle into six equal parts results in three symmetries that can be made visible by shading. It shows the «six-aspect of the one-continuum».

If we look at the circle of the year, we see that it takes just about six full cycles of the moon for a year to «unfold» and another six cycles to complete it.[74] The bees make use of this fact when building their honeycomb in the beehive. In an analogy to the dividing up of the year, each day and night takes six hours to «unfold», and another six to complete.[75]

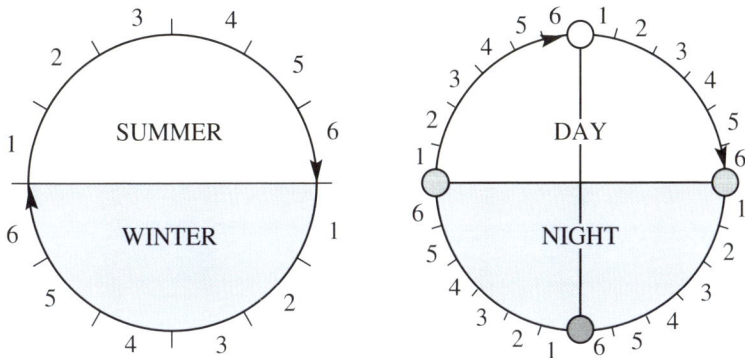

Fig. 117: The «six aspect of the one» is the unfolding of the year in winter/spring and its completion in summer/autumn, or of the day and night.

---

[74] Some 5000 years ago in ancient Egypt this led to the invention of the calendar of twelve months, each one having 30 days (this gives 360 days plus 5 days extra days each year).

[75] See also the *I Ching*, No. 24 and Part 2, Chapter 1 § 1.

From all this we can see that the number six is qualitatively connected to the rhythmical or circular time-bound change in the cosmos, a fact that also becomes visible in the *I Ching*, where with the help of a hexagram (consisting of six full or broken lines) the connection to the «world-clock» of the Tao is established. The six days that God needed to create the cosmos, as told by a Hebrew creation myth, also point to this connection.

Water, the basis of all visible living creation and symbol for cyclical change is also connected to the number six. When water turns into snow, the snow crystals have the following basic structure (see Fig. 118).

On the basis of the amplification given, in a picture, the appearance

Fig. 118: Snow crystals.

of a motif in relation to the number six would point to the *possibility or necessity for a creative joining of the constellated opposites in actual life*. The connection of the six to the two and to the three (2 x 3) would point to an activated fateful content that can or needs to become conscious. As Jung once said: «In creating you are created». If we look at figure 113 again, the six five-petalled red flowers point to a possibility that the woman could keep track of the white man in her actual life with the help of her creative work for the «blue world» beyond. Such loving devotion to the other world was what brought her into analysis.

As later pictures of the same woman show, she tried to realize this possibility by remaining lovingly faithful to her inner fantasy world by carefully noting and painting her dreams and fantasies and trying to understand what all that could mean in her life. In this way she could gradually realize that this white man—who is the same colour as the woman in the picture—was part of her own psyche and was at that time projected onto an outer man, who was for her unattainable. Jung named this inner figure in the woman's psyche the *animus*. It was the woman's creative work on her own fantasies (symbolized by the six) that allowed her to keep in contact with her animus and through this, to start to realize the richness of her soul. There is in the picture a seventh white-red flower that the woman is holding in her hand as if she wanted to offer it to the disappearing man. This leads us to the number seven.

NUMBER 7

Our most common experiences of the number 7 are found in the seven days of the week and the seven natural notes of the scale. After seven days we arrive again at the same day of the week and after seven notes we arrive again at the same note with which we started. It is the same day, the same note, and yet it is not the same: one arrives at the same point as if going through a circle, yet on a different level. That is why the «development by seven steps» has been compared to a spiral.

Mathematically, seven is a prime number. Among the first ten numbers it is the only number that can neither be divided by, nor is it the divisor of any one of them. That is one reason why seven has been considered unique and independent, a sort of «virgin-number». Taken as the sum of 3 and 4, seven is the union of irreversible development in time (3) with the reality of the four elements. It is the number of evolutionary development in the cosmos. For centuries, fate and its development in this world were considered the result of the influence of seven heavenly bodies. Their signs and their ways of influence are summarized in the structure of their symbols. In Western astrology, the basic symbols for the sun, the moon and the earth are combined in various ways to form the symbols of the seven celestial bodies that can be seen from earth by the eye. The circle with the point in the middle symbolizes the sun, the crescent symbolizes the moon, and the cross stands for the earth with its four elements. Thus the symbol of Mercury, for example, represents the union of sun, moon, and earth (see Fig. 119).

 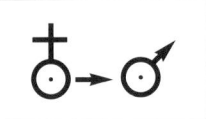

Fig. 119: The symbol for Mercury, is made up of the symbols for sun, moon and earth.

Fig. 120: The symbols of the planets have remained the same since antiquity. Only the symbol for Mars has been modified. The cross has become an arrow.

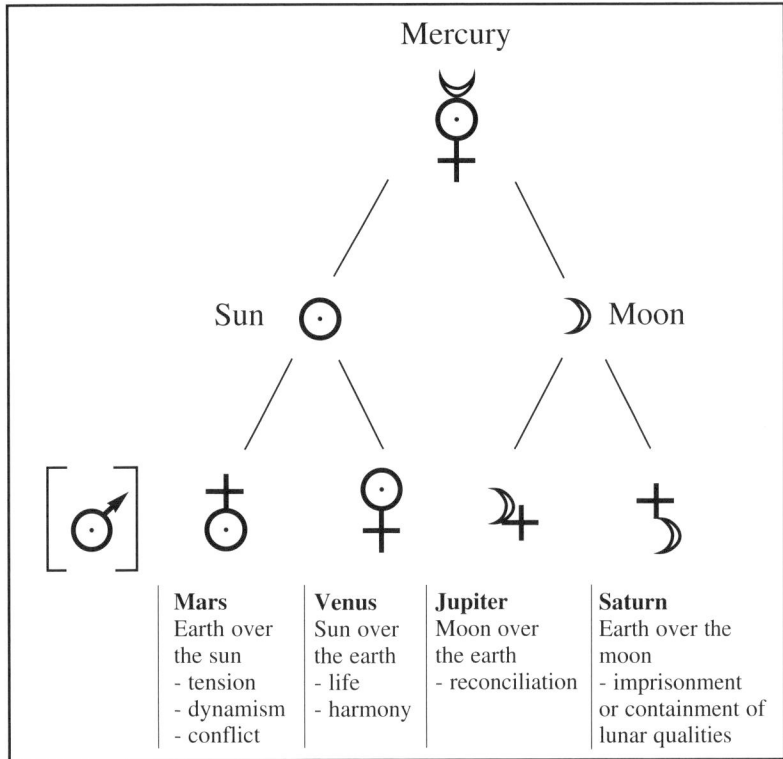

Fig. 121: The 3 + 4 structure of the seven celestial bodies, visible to the eye.[76]

Since the seven days of the week result from dividing the month (as the full circle of the moon) by four, the seven is also connected to all that is influenced by the moon: biological growth, feminine fertility and transformation.[77]

---

[76] For details see R. Allendy, *Le symbolisme des nombres*, p. 172ff.

The fact that human fertility is correlated with the moon cycle points to a fundamental connection of this periodicity to an inner basic human rhythm. As the seven days of the week are very close to one fourth of a moon cycle, the number seven was somehow considered to link with an «inner clock», to our vegetative nervous system that connects us to nature and to natural development.

This connection of the number seven to growth, fertility and transformation is found all over the world, also in the description of *inner growth* and development to completion, to consciousness. There are seven steps to climb in various shamanistic initiations and there are seven hells and seven steps of Purgatory to pass in order to reach heaven, which again brings another seven steps, as described by Dante in his *Divina Comedia*. There are also seven steps to perfection in Buddhism. There is the journey through the seven planets in Mithraism. There are seven steps in alchemy and the seven subtle centres of the charkas in Tantric Yoga. One of the most beautiful examples in literature of the journey of the soul to its purification and the final union with God is found in the book named *Haf Pakar* (Persian = the seven pictures) written by the Persian mystic Nizami. The journey of the soul is described in seven stories told to the hero by seven different princesses. These stories are told on the seven days of one week.

As we have seen, the number six is related to the circle, the completeness of the circle. The number seven can be understood as the *septa-essentia* of the six but also as the number that goes beyond the six of the complete circle (see Fig. 122).[78] For that reason the 7 is—like the 13 that goes beyond the completeness of the circle with 12 divisions—a fateful number. Either it leads to further development and is then a *creative number* or it leads to hybris and is then associated with *evil forces*. (For the

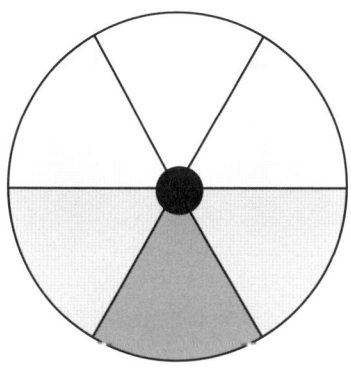

Fig. 122:
The «seven-aspect of the one-continuum».

---

[77] It is remarkable that $1 + 2 + 3 + 4 + 5 + 6 + 7 = 28$, is the number close to the days from one full moon to the next.
[78] For instance in the six double months of the ancient Islamic calendar.

Japanese the 7 is an unlucky number as is the 13 for many people in Western culture.) For many people the is however, a lucky number with magic power.[79]

Looking at the quality of the number seven, we can sum up by saying that the «seven-aspect of the one» points to the force beyond the circular movement of the six. Thus the seven leads to a basic rhythm in nature that in the outer world is connected to music and moon-time, whereas in humans the number seven seems to be connected to man's unconscious soul and his spiritual development. Whenever the number seven appears in a picture or a dream, we can assume that the *possibility or need for spiritual development or transformation is activated,* a development in the direction of higher consciousness, towards individuation.

Our next picture (see Fig. 123), a woodcarving done by a 24-year-old man, was created because he saw it just like this in his dream and felt

Fig. 123: Woodcarving done by a 24-year-old man (see also Fig. 57 on p. 78).

---

[79] Even in ancient Egypt one had to repeat a spell seven times. Apophis, the evil serpent, had to be cut in seven parts in the seventh hour of the Amduat, a book for the afterlife.

[80] See, for instance, in C.G. Jung, *Mysterium Coniunctionis* [Coll. Works 14], Chapter 3e Personification of the Opposites: Ascent and Descent, § 290f.

a need to bring it to reality. It shows the passing of the «sun-child» through the houses of the planets, starting with the moon on which the sun-child is sitting. The six other planets are represented by the round arches, which have within them unusual signs for the planets. At that time the dreamer had not the faintest idea that the picture of his dream represented an archetypal idea of spiritual development that we find, for instance, in alchemy.[80]

The picture shown in figure 124 was painted by a 32-year-old

Fig. 124: Drawn by a 32-year-old woman.

146 Number Symbolism

woman, after accepting an «unorthodox fantasy». It also shows seven steps up to an unknown area that hints at a connection to some feminine mystery. The whole area is surrounded by intense fire. The striking analogy to an alchemical picture of the *Museum Hermeticum* (see Fig. 125) was very surprising to the woman and gave her confidence in the process that was triggered off when she accepted her fantasy.

Fig. 125: Alchemical picture from S. Mittelspacher, *Cabala* (1654).

In figure 113 (on p. 137), which we have already looked at, the six red flowers, together with the seventh larger white flower, also point to such a spiritual development, which was activated by the longing of consciousness to connect with the ghostly lover.

Now the step from the seven to the eight represents the same problem as the step from the three to the four, only on a more differentiated level. From the seven to the eight it is only half a step, compared to the one from three to four. While seven represents the ability of the soul to develop, eight points to the goal of this development, which we will now examine more closely.

Number 8

Mathematically the number 8 is a doubled four. It therefore carries qualities similar to the four, but on a more differentiated level. The «eight aspect of the one» introduces the symmetry of the «four aspect of the one» on a more subtle level that suggests the possibility of conscious assimilation of the totality (= the four) of the one-continuum. As we can see in the illustration of the double crosswise division of the circle (Fig. 126), the eight appears as the number of the just-so-ness of complete divine cosmic order, or in other words, of fuller orientation within the wholeness of the circle, differentiating each quadrant into both its darker and its lighter aspect.

The eight-fold wheel in Buddhism, the eight triples in the Chinese *I Ching* or the medicine wheel of the American Indians, are illustrations of this archetypal image.

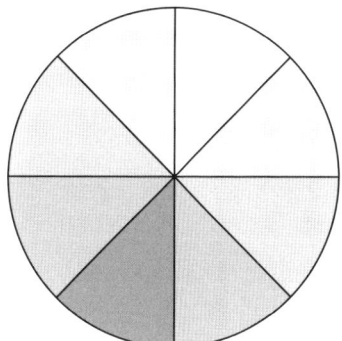

Fig. 126: The «eight-aspect of the one-continuum» with four symmetries making the darker and lighter part of each quadrant visible.

As the sum of 7 + 1, the eight makes the completion of the development by seven steps. In this way the eight became associated with the «inner sun» or the «mountain of bliss», the goal of the journey through the seven planets in alchemy or in Mithraism. In medieval European belief, the eight stands for the realm of the fixed stars, the sphere that transcends the fateful dependence on the influence of the seven planets. In this context, the eight was associated with Christ, who was considered to be the destroyer of the bondage to the planets and whose resurrection took place on the eighth day. Because of this, the eight was an emblem of the waters of baptism in the Middle Ages.

Psychologically, we can understand the eight as a symbol for the possibility or the need for consciousness as a result of an inner development. The journey of the soul (seven steps) in the vessel of the psyche gives birth to the inner new light, the *deus in homine*. As completion of the seven steps, the eight is also connected to the realm beyond time and death, to the immortal soul and to eternity, a fact that we can see in the mathematical symbol for infinity ∞ that is a horizontal 8. As symmetry of the four aspect of the one, the eight points to a totality that can be or has to be recognized in its light and dark aspect.

On the basis of all this, the eight-fold structure in pictures indicates that whatever is connected to this number points to the psychological goal of human life, namely the development of consciousness that should or can be recognized and cultivated. Often in periods of disorientation, an eight-fold mandala (as these images are called in India) comes up from the unconscious to convey the message that there is a supreme order and meaning in the background of the soul, in spite of the chaos on the surface. Figure 127 shows such a mandala. It gives us the impression of a divine appearance, a unifying force that reconciles the opposites of modern civilization and nature. This unifying function used to be attributed especially to the octagon.[81]

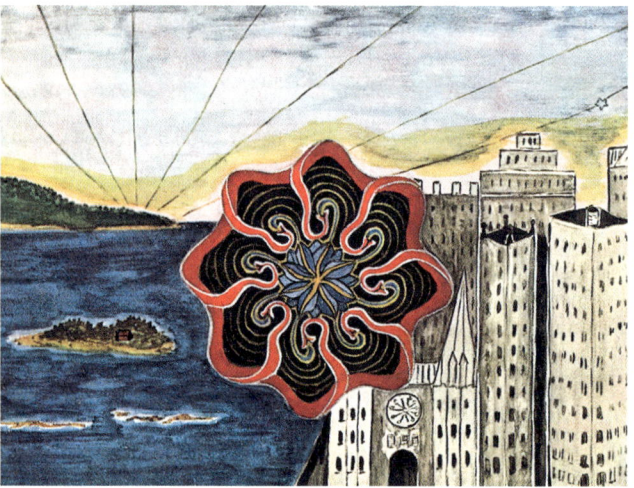

Fig. 127: Eight-fold mandala as symbol for the Self that can create a peaceful inner union of the extreme opposites of nature and modern city life.[82]

---

[81] M. Khanna, *Yantra, the Tantric Symbol of Cosmic Unity*.
[82] C.G. Jung, *Archetype and the Collective Unconscious* [Coll. Works 9, I], Chapter: A Study in the Process of Individuation, §525–626, Fig. 15.

NUMBER 9

After the completion of the eight, the number 9 as 8 + 1 represents a new beginning. This aspect we still find clearly in the French word for nine: *neuf* also means new. The German word for nine, *neun*, is also closely connected to the German word *neu*, new.[83] The nine, when looked at as being generated from 3 x 3, can be understood as the potentiated dynamism of the three. In the Middle Ages this was the reason why the nine was associated with the all-pervading Holy Ghost.[84] Yet it would again be one-sided to conclude from this dynamism that the nine has only masculine qualities. There is a strong receptive feminine element linked to the nine as well. It takes nine months from conception to the birth of a child, and thus for the Mayans, for instance, the nine was the holy number of the moon-goddess.[85]

When looked at as a means of summarizing what went before, the nine shows the union of the eight—a quality comparable to the five—*as «quinta essentia»* of the four. Therefore we can understand the nine as the unifying principle of the unfolded cosmic order on a *more differentiated* conscious level. Nine would therefore be the navel point of the cosmic wheel. We could call it the *nona-essentia* of the eight aspect of a differentiated consciousness, symbolized by the eight.

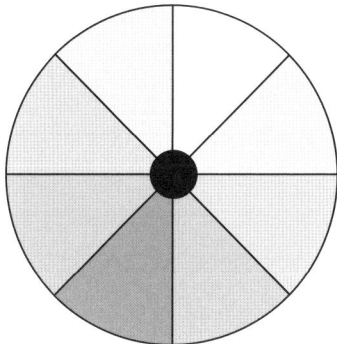

Fig. 128: The unifying ninth element of the cosmic wheel, the *nona-essentia* of the eight.

---

[83] In Greek *ennéa* is connected to *néos*, in latin *noven* to *novum*.
[84] See V.F. Hopper, *Medieval Number Symbolism*, p. 122ff.
[85] For details see J. Chevalier and A. Gheerbrant, *Dictionnaire des Symboles*, Chapter 9 (*neuf*).

From the connection of the nine with the five we can understand why in courtly love the nine symbolized the mystery of spiritualized eros. For Dante, the nine was his adored number in relation to his love for Beatrice, his soul-guide: «The nine was her true Self» as he said.[86]

The three, as union of the opposites and as child of yin and yang, stands for synthesis. The nine, consisting of *three triplets*, has a similar uniting quality, but on a higher level. The arrangement of 3 x 3 makes up a square (see Fig. 129).

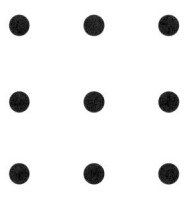

1	2	3
4	5	6
7	8	9

Fig. 129: Nine as three times three triplets. The nine is the last simple number.

Besides the quality of dynamism and what goes beyond the number 8, the number 9, being the last simple number, also marks an end. The number 9 was therefore considered to represent the last step of a cosmogonic development, especially in relationship to human culture, meaning higher consciousness. After all, human beings are carried in the womb of their mother for 9 months. The connection of the number 9 to human culture is found in different myths: for nine days and nine nights Odin hung on the world tree to afterwards bring the runes—the ancient German alphabet—to humanity in nine songs. It took Leto nine days (meaning nine circles of the sun) to give birth to Diana and Apollo, the latter being the god of human culture. Apollo was accompanied by nine Muses, who represent the totality of human knowledge and culture. From all this we can sum up the qualities of the «nine-aspect of the one». It is a *creative, transformative and unifying dynamism that seems to be mysteriously connected to the development of human consciousness.*

The appearance of a motif connected to the number 9 in a picture or a dream would point to *the possibility or the need to differentiate creatively that particular aspect* in order that its uniting dynamism can become conscious and enter life. In its essence it is a spiritual problem that leads finally to the possibility of a development towards a further differentiated personality that will be at one with itself and the world.

---

[86] See Dante Alighieri, *La vita nuova*, pp. 26–27.

Number Symbolism 151

The following picture (Fig. 130), painted by the same 34-year-old woman who created the picture of the number 5 (Fig. 112), was painted as the third in a row. (Her first picture was on the number 3, the second on the number 6.) It shows the emerging of the number 9 from the mouth of the beautiful fish in the depths of the sea. The stars in the sea recall a low sky with the archetypes (= the stars) having a bodily aspect. From this area of the body and its instincts, the number 9 comes to the surface of consciousness in this young woman. It symbolizes a surfacing of a new and more differentiated awareness of the numinous quality of the mystery of beauty and creativity, which in the beginning of her analysis was understood in too concrete a way. This awareness finally led to the picture of the number 5, the centre of figure 112 on page 136.

Fig. 130: Painted by a woman at the age of 34.

NUMBER 10

With the number 10 we arrive at the limit of counting with our fingers. By this natural means of counting, ten became the basis of our decimal system, which starts counting again after ten (10 + 1 = 11 and so on). At the same time, the ten is also the sum of the first four numbers: 1 + 2 + 3 + 4 = 10. Because of this, the ten was the most holy number for the Pythagoreans, symbolizing the creation of the world. They represented the ten, as sum of the first four numbers, in the form of a triangle (Tetraktys, see Fig. 131).

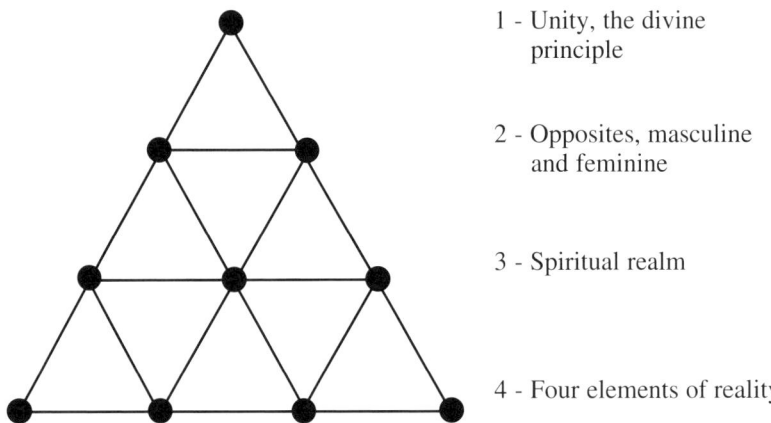

1 - Unity, the divine principle

2 - Opposites, masculine and feminine

3 - Spiritual realm

4 - Four elements of reality

Fig. 131: The Tetraktys of the Pythagoreans.[87]

In summary we can say that the ten becomes the reappearance of the one, uniting all the nine numbers. As such, it is the reappearance or the coming together of the whole of creation, including human consciousness. Looked at it this way, the ten carries the quality of embracing the whole variety of creation to become a multiple unity. In psychological language, we would speak of a symbol of the Self that contains, centres and regulates the many different archetypes.

This unifying quality of the number was especially alive in the alchemical tradition, where it became a symbol for the «Stone of the Sages,» the lapis. The ten corresponds to the sum of the four steps of the alchemists' work to produce this lapis, the four steps that were identical with the first four numbers.[88] As ten multiplies easily, the *multiplicatio*, meaning the multiplying influence of the lapis on its surroundings, was represented as a multiplication of the ten to 100, 1000, etc.

---

[87] See C. Butler, *Number Symbolism*, pp. 1–10 (on Greek Origins of Number Symbolism, the Pythagoreans).

[88] See C.G. Jung, *Psychology and Alchemy* [*Collected Works* 12], § 333–335. The Pythagoreans considered ten as their most holy number. Von Franz comments on the Tetraktys in *Number and Time,* p. 114.

Number Symbolism

Ten as a symbol for Christ, the Gnostic anthropos or the Cabalistic Sefirot tree are further illustrations of the completing, all-uniting and radiating quality of the ten.

Fig. 132: The Gnostic *anthropos* as a god-like being. He is uniting in the ten the four elements, 1 standing for earth, 2 for water, 3 for air and 4 for fire. He is not only the master of the day world of the sun but also of the dark night of the moon below.[89]

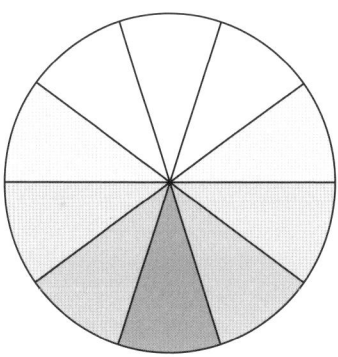

Fig. 133: The «ten-aspect of the one-continuum» shown in five symmetries.

---

[89] J. J. Mangetus, *Bibliotheca Chymica Curiosa*, Vol. I, 13, p. 938.

The appearance of the number 10 in a picture or a dream would therefore point to the possibility or the need for a coming together of all the different aspects of life. As a symbol for individuation it can point out that reconciliation with the inner pattern of wholeness is now activated. The following alchemical picture (Fig. 134) illustrates how the old king—in alchemy as well as in fairy tales, a symbol for a worn-out attitude that is no longer in direct contact with the wholeness of life—is attacked and destroyed by ten peasants, who represent that inner possibility for wholeness that is in close contact with nature. In alchemy, the tenth was also the earth, reality in its wholeness, which is united to the three other elements (4 [= fire] + 3 [= air] + 2 [=water]).[90]

Fig. 134: From D. Stoltzius von Stoltzenberg, *Viridarium Chymicum*, LXXXVIII.

---

[90] See M.-L. von Franz, *Aurora Consurgens*, p. 251.

d. Numbers from 11 to 17

For numbers from 11 to 17 there will be, except for the number 12, a brief amplification.

NUMBER 11

Taken as the sum of 10 + 1, the number 11 is the first number that goes beyond the perfect order of the totality of the ten. This brings the number close to the quality of the two, a quality that was seen confirmed by the fact that the sign for eleven (11) is made up of two ones: 1+1 = 2. This explains the origin of the rather bad reputation that the eleven has in Christian tradition; there it became the number of the devil, of sin (the going beyond the ten commandments), of excess, conflict, hubris and sickness. Through that, the eleven became connected to man, who can disobey the cosmic order and go beyond it. However, considering that the «eleven-aspect of the one» is the unity of the 10, we can see that limiting the eleven to the hybris-quality is inappropriate. The eleven is *also* the essence of the five-fold symmetry of the one (see Fig. 135). This aspect of the number 11

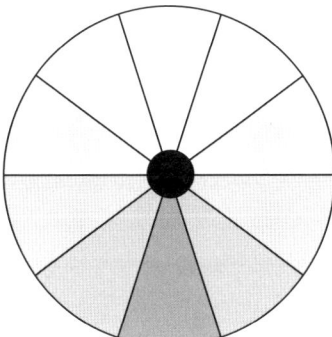

Fig. 135: The «eleven-aspect of the one», the unity of the ten in the one.

was already seen this way in ancient China. For the Chinese, the eleven was, in a retrospective way, the unity of the decade in its wholeness.[91] They considered this number as the number of Tao, being the sum of the five (microcosm) and the six (macrocosm).

---

[91] See M.-L. von Franz, *Number and Time*, p. 65.

Number 12

As a doubled six, the number 12 is closely related to the circle and all that we have seen in relation to the number 6. Since twelve moon cycles make up a year—our twelve months and the twelve zodiac signs—the number 12 is connected to solar time. For that the daily circle of the sun is divided into 2 x 12 hours as well.

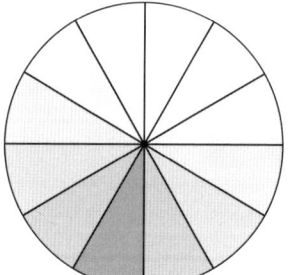

Fig. 136: The «twelve-aspect of the one» showing six symmetries.

In Pharaonic Egypt, the renewal of the sun god from the old sun at the time of sunset to the rejuvenated sun god at the time of sunrise took place by his passing through the 12 hours of the night. The knowledge of the sun god's successful nightly journey to his own daily renewal is described in the royal books of the afterlife. They were considered to contain important knowledge for the deceased Pharaoh for his own immortality. In that night-journey of the sun god through the 12 hours of the night we recognize today a symbolic description of the renewal of human consciousness by the night-world, the unconscious. Today this is experienced in the healing process in a psychic crisis or illness, such as depression.[92]

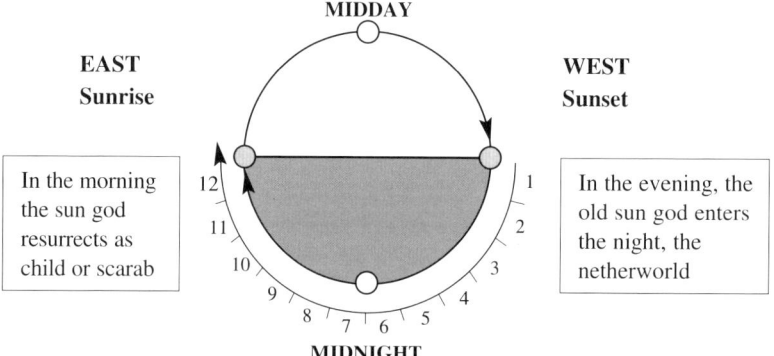

Fig. 137: Night-journey of the Pharaonic sun god through the twelve hours of the night.

---

[92] See T. Abt and E. Hornung, *Knowledge for the Afterlife*, Zurich 2003.

Number Symbolism

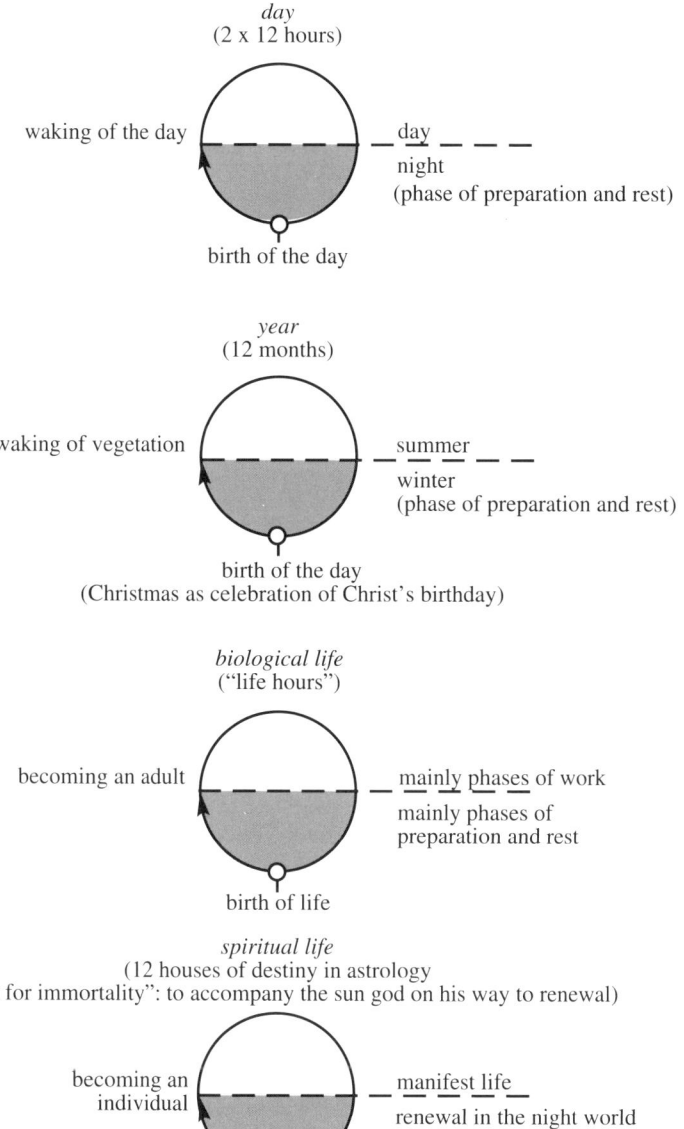

Fig. 138: The daily circle of the sun and the signified development of humans.

158   Number Symbolism

We looked at the picture shown in figure 139 when focusing on the colour black on page 105. Out of the woman's depression this mandala emerged. When we now focus on the number symbolism of this picture, we see the numbers 4 and 12 are quite prominent: the four bird-like beings with four lines ending in a little ball and then the black four triple-rings; next, towards the centre, we see 12 yellow-brown parts of something resembling a spinning wheel that encircles a centre that again is encircled by a black snake. The red-black centre is as if touched by the tongue of the

Fig. 139: Drawn by a woman at the age of 32 (see also Fig. 46, p. 70).

snake. The mystery of the centre seems protected or vitalized by this wheel made of 12 parts. This points to a concentration of the inner energies that gravitate around this one central issue, characterized by a four-fold structure. One could understand this dynamism of the number 12 as a need or a possibility to activate the inner centre by all the aspects or qualities of time, such as the 12 signs of the zodiac or the 12 double hours of the day. Indeed, the further work with this woman showed her commitment to her psyche, which led to the creation of many more pictures. (See also figure 69 on page 91.)

The number 12 is created by 3 x 4. For that, this number was considered a reconciliation number, namely by the fact that it brings together the number 3 as fateful dynamism in time with the completed orientation pattern of the number 4.⁹³

In figure 140, painted by a 32-year-old woman, we see an enigmatic three-layered flying object in the sky, with twelve people arranged in three groups of four. They are somehow suspended in space between the four people in the car on the ground and the three lens-shaped flying objects in the top right-hand corner of the sky. The central symbol can be understood as an attempt for a union of the earthy reality, symbolised by the four persons on earth, and the heavenly uncanny dynamism, symbolised by the three flying lenses. The reconciling symbol is a three-dimensional mandala that contains 3 x 4 = 12 human beings. Such a mandala is in general an attempt at a higher union of the opposites. This vision seems to point to the possibility of a reconciliation of the extra-worldly reality (the UFOs) with the reality we live in.⁹⁴

Fig. 140: Painted by a 32-year-old woman (see also Fig. 113 on p. 137).

---

93   In the book of Revelations, the number 12 appears in the twelve gates of the heavenly Jerusalem and in the twelve stars of the crown of the woman, who stands on both sun and moon, the 144,000 followers (12 x 12 x 1000) etc.The Bible, Book of Revelations, 12 and 21.

94   More on this can be found in C.G. Jung's text on flying saucers: C.G. Jung, «A Modern Myth of Things Seen in the Sky» [Coll. Works 10], § 589ff.

Number 13

As 12 + 1 the number 13 is again, like the numbers 5, 7, 9 and 11, a number that goes beyond a given totality, this time beyond the dozen. Because of this, in Christianity it was—similar to the number eleven—considered a fateful number. Going beyond the circle of time given by the creator, in Christianity it mainly connoted sin, hybris and so forth. As such, it was and still is generally considered an unlucky number. But on the other hand, the thirteen for Christians is also connected to Jesus, the focal point of his twelve apostles. Thus thirteen either represents Jesus, followed by his twelve apostles; or negatively, the thirteen represents Judas, together with the twelve others, the eleven other apostles and Jesus.

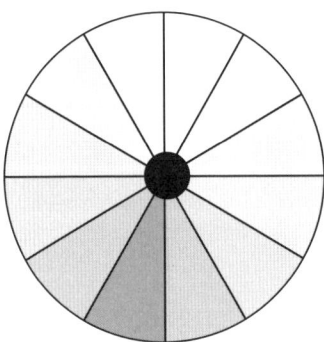

With regard to the «thirteen-aspect of the one-continuum» it is the unity or essence of the twelve, the unity of the complete circle of the twelve as a wholeness. This aspect is represented, for instance, in alchemy in the sun–moon tree, where the sun unites the twelve signs of the zodiac, the twelve moons or months. As such a unity, the thirteen represents the wholeness of the complete dynamism of the cosmos (see Fig. 141). Figure 142 shows the birth of the new sun as the child of the twelve months.

Fig. 141: The «thirteen-aspect of the one-continuum», the essence of the twelve.

Fig. 142: The thirteen in alchemy.[95]

---

[95] D. Stoltzius von Stoltzenberg, *Viridarium Chymicum*, LXX.

Number Symbolism

Fig. 143: Picture by a 22-year-old man. (See also figures 59 and 86, pages 80 and 105.)

The central content of this sketch-like picture (Fig. 143) is the black transparent wand (as the author of the picture called it) on a red mandorla-shaped background that contains a feminine figure. It divides the picture into two halves, a lower yellow one and a black upper one. Everything is focused on her. This reveals the central love-problem of this young man: a bewitched woman, who, like Snow White lies in a transparent container. In the lower right corner we see three yellow, fully drawn bows. This points to a fateful dynamism that comes from the area of the lower, bodily drives. The thirteen yellow lines, which look as though they are parts of a circle, could indicate some sort of disturbance since they go beyond the "normal circle" of the twelve, possibly symbolizing the inexplicable way in which the painter was "possessed". In the upper left corner we see a dwarf with a hood. He is pointing with a stick towards the central content, the woman. That could be a gesture of threatening or redeeming this woman. The mercurial dwarf or wizard is surrounded by fourteen lines pointing in the same direction as his stick. This could be interpreted as the possibility of or the need for a regulating "upper" spiritual energy which comes from the "black, unconscious world". The dynamism that comes from the yellow area of "lower" bodily drives is regulated by being given a meaning that, with the dwarf's hood and its moon and stars, is linked to the archetypal world. The rather cool and feminine green and blue colours are completely missing in the picture. The man who did this painting did indeed need to see the archetypal background of his conflict and to reflect on it. This enabled him to realize that this picture was revealing to him his basic task in life: to redeem his anima, his feminine side, which had been "bewitched".

NUMBER 14

It takes fourteen days to pass from the new moon to the full moon. This closely connects the number 14 (like the number 7) to the moon and its qualities. The «fourteen-aspect of the one continuum» is the unity of the thirteen and as such, the consolidation of the step beyond the twelve. In this way, the fourteen represents the consolidation of a development of consciousness on which the individual can rely. We find this quality of the number 14 expressed, for instance, in the Catholic folk-belief of the fourteen helpers in need (German = *Nothelfer*) or the fourteen Ka that accompanied the Pharaoh when he travelled. They represented his connection to the archetypal basis of his personality, his bridge to the collective unconscious. The grouping of the ancestors of Jesus in units of fourteen demonstrates the same idea.[96] The fourteen lions in figure 144 illustrate the foundation of the mysterious conjunction of sun-king and moon-queen: the differentiated 7 (2 x 7), as the wholeness of the light and the dark side of the development of consciousness, which can give birth to a new light that results from the union of the opposites (see Fig. 145).

Fig. 144: The fourteen lions in alchemy.[97]

---

[96] See the Bible, Matthew 1.
[97] D. Stoltzius von Stoltzenberg, *Viridarium Chymicum*, XXXXVII.

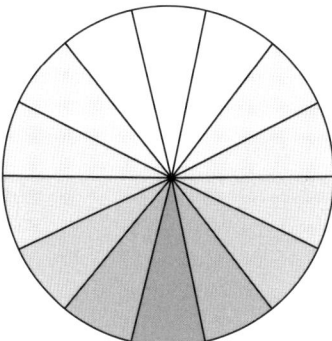

Fig. 145: The «fourteen-aspect of the one-continuum» with seven symmetries (7 x 2) as the main characteristic of the number 14.

NUMBER 15

The number 15 has quite a remarkable quality, which is comparable to the number 10. It is the sum of the first five numbers, 1 + 2 + 3 + 4 + 5 = 15. Yet it is not only the sum of the adding up of our main counting device, the five fingers; it is also, in a remarkable way, related to the first nine numbers. If we arrange the nine ciphers in a square, the so-called magic square, the sum of three numbers in all directions is always fifteen, as the diagram below shows (see Fig. 146).

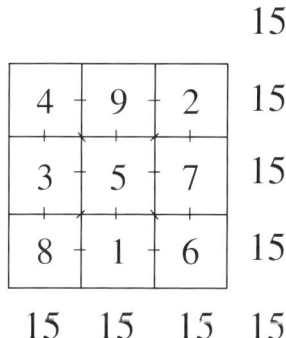

Fig. 146: The so-called magic square made up of the first nine ciphers. The sum of all the rows—horizontally, vertically and diagonally—results in the number 15.

Looked at qualitatively, fifteen is the union or the essence of the number 14; this would represent the whole range of manifest creation that carries consciousness. As such, with the fifteen we reach a boundary that is at the same time a door to the beyond, and thus is comparable to the seven. Yet on another level, the step from the number 15 to 16 is smaller than the step from 7 to 8 or, as we have seen earlier, from 3 to 4. With this we reach the sixteen, the second last number that we shall amplify.

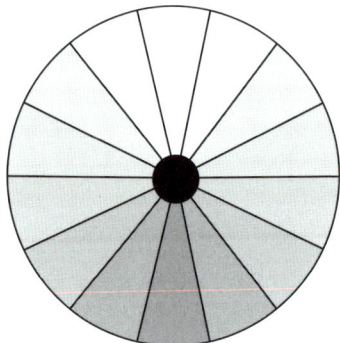

Fig. 147: The «fifteen-aspect of the one-continuum» the unity of the 14.

NUMBER 16

The number 16 is four times four (4 x 4) and thus closely related to the quality of the number 4. It can be understood as a completely differentiated realization (i.e. with all the four functions of consciousness) of the «four-aspect of the one».

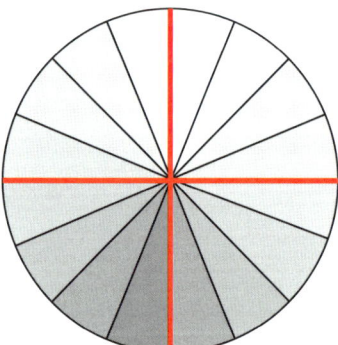

Fig. 148: The «sixteen-aspect of the one-continuum» is the symmetry of the number 8 or the double symmetry of the number 4.

Number 17

The quality of the «seventeen-aspect of the one» can be understood as the essence of the number 16. The number 5 was the essence of the number 4, the quintessence. Now the number 17 has the quality of being the essence of the four parts of the circle *with each part being as such completely recognized with all the four functions.* This enables us to understand why in the Orient the number 17 symbolized a clear limit. This quality of the number 17 was recognized in the Bible[98] and later by the Shiites. For them the number 17 is a most holy number, connected to the mystery of Allah's presence in matter,[99] especially for the famous Arab alchemist Jabir Ibn Hayyan, who said: «Know that everything on earth—I mean in the world of becoming and of perishing—will not pass beyond the seventeen power-units».[100]

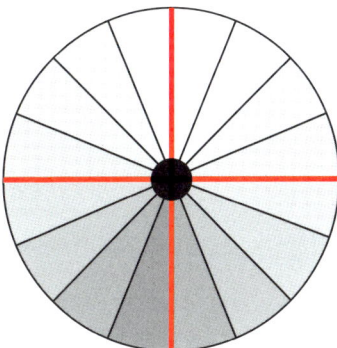

Fig. 149: The number 17 as the quintessence of the four parts of the one circle. All four parts are again fully differentiated into four, a symbol for complete recognition by the four aspects of consciousness, the four functions. Thus the number 17 has the quality of a limit to conscious recognition of the world.

---

[98] The flood started on the 17th day of the second month and ended on the 17th day of 17th month. Noah's Ark seems to be connected somehow to the number 17.
[99] Ğābir Ibn Ḥayyān, *The Book of the Concentration*, pp. 121–123.
[100] See F.C. Endres and A. Schimmel, *Das Mysterium der Zahl*, p. 236f.

3.7. Motifs

The amplification of the different motifs, as far as they are recognizable as such, is the most obvious element in picture interpretation. It needs, however, the same knowledge that is required for understanding dream motifs. The tree, the egg, the circle, the house, the fire etc. are all symbols that express in the best possible way something otherwise not understandable. They are not simply signs expressing for instance «nothing but ...» a sexual organ. Each element of a picture will contribute to making the whole picture become alive, if only we let these different motifs express themselves by our amplification work. The relationship of the different motifs to formal aspects, space, colour and number symbolism will clarify the meaning of these motifs.

Fig. 150: Picture by a 27-year-old man (see also Fig. 40).

The black circle and the pink spiral form connected to the green form below are in the left half of the picture (see Fig. 150), while the blue line with clearly shaped angles and the brown–orange coloured triangular shape with the parallel lines are in the right half of the picture. The round forms, symbols of elements also found in nature, are quite disconnected from the constucted forms of the conscious mind of this young student of psychology. These round forms, the circle as a symbol for wholeness and the spiral as symbol for the possibility of self-unfolding or development, are connected to the colour black and a very light red, almost pink. These inner realities are completely disconnected from the «world on the right side». The blue line, which is broken four times, and the orange triangular form with its parallel lines symbolize how this world is intellectually constructed. There is no life in it and the orange of the triangular form points rather to an aggressive tone connected to this construction. The young man was absorbed by his studies in psychology, but he was not so interested in understanding individual human beings. He was rather fascinated by statistical studies, where humans are reduced to abstract units. His own natural side suffered from this disconnection. That was the reason for consulting me.

Our next example (Fig. 151) is of a dream (see also Fig. 21, p. 43) drawn in black and white by a 28-year-old woman.

Fig. 151: Dream text and picture by a 28-year-old woman. The French text of the dream reads: «A woman and a man, wearing medieval clothes, carry a big white egg. They intend to put it between two objects, resembling loudspeakers, which will ventilate it in order that it [the egg] can be aired».

The next picture (Fig. 152) emerged three years later and shows what was born out of the mysterious egg that needed first to be ventilated by air, a symbol for exposure to the spirit of the unconscious. The egg had to be put in the vessel of the analytic work and relationship and exposed to «the right measure of the fire» as we can read in different alchemical texts. This means that the emotional involvement has to be neither too hot nor too cold so that it does not to burn up or freeze the living content of the egg. What is then born out of the egg is a winged insect, an image of something entirely different from our conscious human existence. Such an insect is a well-known symbol for the living experience of the divine-other in humans. It is known for example in the symbol of the scarab in ancient Egypt or the mantis of the Kalahari Bushmen in South Africa or the grasshopper, the so called Lightning Man, of the Aborigines in Kakadu in the Northern Territory of Australia.

Fig. 152: Painted by the same person as for figure 151.

3.8. Potential Criteria for Latent Psychosis

For an analyst it is important to be able to sense the possibility of the danger of a latent psychosis. An overly optimistic attitude can lead to a «participation mystique» with a client, seducing them into a dangerous dive into the unconscious that might threaten his or her ego-stability. There are different criteria in a picture that can hint at such a danger. In order to make it possible in practical work to apply these criteria, it is preferable briefly to look at some basic points. For details I refer to some detailed research on these different criteria.[101]

The following general criteria may mirror a weak or unstable ego, *but* the same criteria may also appear in a picture at times of transition of a personality, where the ego has to be dissolved by the forces of the unconscious in order to re-adapt to the archetypal reality and by that to be renewed. As always, it depends on the whole context of the picture, whether or not we consider a situation in a picture as pointing to some psychological danger.

1. Lack of homogeneity in the picture
a. Rupture in the style: For instance there is a landscape and all of a sudden there is a completely different style in one part of the picture. This can point to an ego that is not strong enough to maintain a consistent style (see Fig. 153 on the next page).

But it can also mirror a strong upheaval in a certain area of the psyche, for which another style is its appropriate symbolic expression. (See Fig. 90 on p. 114.)

b. Rupture in the perspective: This can indicate an inability of the ego to maintain a consistent standpoint throughout the picture. One part is seen from this standpoint, another from another one (see Fig. 153 on the next page).

But it can also point to an emotional upheaval that is so bewildering that a change of the perspective is just vital.

2. Lack of a firm standpoint
a. A high horizon: This can point either to a lack of a balanced view of the upper part with the lower part *or* it can be understood as weakness of the ego, not able to free itself from being caught in a concrete situation (see Fig. 154 on the next page and Fig. 83 on p. 101).

But it can also mirror a need for an overview.

---

[101] H. Prinzhorn, *Artistry of the Mentally Ill*, 1995; H. Rennert, *Merkmale schizophrener Bildnerei*, 1962; A. Bader, *Wahn und Wirklichkeit*, 1976.

Fig. 153: Painting by a 40-year-old man.

Fig. 154: Painting by a 28-year-old man.

b. Cut-off motifs: Using these can point to a weak ego that is not able to arrange the elements within a set frame (see Fig. 155).

But it can also mirror very strong contents that cannot yet be properly integrated within the totality of the psyche.

Fig. 155: Painting by a 24-year-old man, the same person who painted figure 83 on page 101. The cut-off motif of the claw points to the absolutely overwhelning force from a daemonic spirit-bird.

3. Lack of centring function

Oscillation of lines, up and down: This can point to an autonomous continuation of the «yes» and «no» that we find when the ego is not able to hold the tension of the opposites and is being forced to swing with them, so to speak. (See Fig. 95 on p. 121.) *But* it can also point to a state before the birth of something new, the third, where the «yes» and «no» can be experienced in its full intensity.

Part 4

Some Final Considerations

Fig. 156: This picture by a 35-year-old man originated from a dream and a following active imagination. It shows the collaboration of the unconscious with consciousness, out of which this symbol was born. Out of each of the four elements—*terra* (= earth), *aqua* (= water), *aer* (= air) and *ignis* (= fire) at the bottom—a tree is growing. And out of these four trees one light is coming into existence as the fifth, the quintessence. This central light appears to have a face, connecting it to a human head or consciousness. The picture is surrounded by a black snake that bites its tail. It is separating or protecting the emerging light that comes out of this natural symbolic process. The picture can be understood as a *symbol of the process of the creation of consciousness.* It can also been seen as an illustration of the process of distilling, out from or with the four functions of consciousness, the one meaning of a picture, dream, fairy tale or myth. Out of this circumambulating process the meaning of a picture or symbolic story can grow and gradually become conscious. We can understand this picture as a symbol, i.e. the best possible representation of something otherwise not representable, of what I understand by *illuminating a picture from the unconscious with its own light.*

4. Some Final Considerations

At the end of our journey of seeking a way to interpret pictures from the unconscious, we can sit back and reflect a little on what has been been developed.

We started by noticing a first reaction to a picture. Then we tried to circumambulate the picture for a first time with our four functions, in order to arrive at a hypothesis as well as a counter-hypothesis. This act we compared to a first living cell (see page 50). Then we continued with the second part of the work, further differentiating the four functions in such a way that they grow towards the centre, evaluating our hypothesis and counter-hypothesis. This would make it possible to clarify which of the two assumptions would prove to be the more plausible. When we consider this process in the light of earlier traditions that were trying to create consciousness, we find some striking parallels.

Arabic alchemy, which was developed in the 10th century to a remarkably high degree, had a similar approach for the cultivation of gold (*zirā'at aḍ-ḍahab*), as they called this work in Arabic. In a treatise attributed to Cleopatra, we read that first an egg has to be produced by uniting the four elements. That is a potentially living unit; it is the first part of the work. Then, in the second part of the work, this egg has to be hatched to become alive. This hatching is a symbol for thinking or pondering intensively, as we can read in these achemical texts.

The egg would correspond to the union achieved by the pondering over the picture from the unconscious with the four functions of consciousness. This leads to a hypothesis and a counter-hypothesis (the *albedo* or «making white» in alchemy). The second part of the work—the hatching of the egg that would finally allow a living bird (= spirit) to emerge out of the egg—would correspond to allowing the picture to reveal a living understanding of its meaning (the *rubedo* or «making red» in alchemy). This shows that our method of trying to create consciousness out of pictures from the unconscious, a method that is based on the psychology of C.G. Jung, was already somehow known to the old masters of alchemy.

In the meantime the method proposed here has also been applied successfully to the interpretation of dreams, fairy tales and myths. This experience has been confirmed in the work of a number of students at the Research and Training Centre for Depth Psychology according to C.G. Jung and Marie-Louise von Franz.

---

[1] Especially by masters like Ğābir Ibn Hayyān and Muḥammad Ibn Umail.
[2] See M. Ullmann, «Kleopatra in einer arabischen alchemistischen Disputation», p. 173.

Bibliography

ABT, Theodor. *The Great Vision of Muḥammad Ibn Umail*. Supplement to Psychological Perspectives, Los Angeles 2003.
- and HORNUNG, Erik. *Knowledge for the Afterlife,* Zurich 2003.
- *Number Symbolism*, private edition, Zurich 1988.

Abu al-Qāsim al-'Irāqī, Muḥammad b. Aḥmad. The Acquired Knowledge Concerning the Cultivation of Gold, Paris 1923.

ALIGHIERI, Dante. *La vita nuova,* Firenze, Sermartelli 1576.

ALLENDY, René. *Le symbolisme des nombres, essai d'arithmosophie,* Paris 1921, reprint of 2nd edition (Paris 1948), Paris 1984.

BACH, Susan. *Life paints its own Span*, Einsiedeln 1995.

BADER, Alfred. *Zwischen Wahn und Wirklichkeit. Kunst, Psychose, Kreativität*, Luzern 1976.

BENNET, E.A. "Aus dem Vorwort–von E.A. Bennet", in: C.G. Jung, *Das Symbolische Leben, Gesammelte Werke* 18/I, Solothurn, Düsseldorf 1981.

The Bible (Old and New Testament).

BRUTSCHE, Paul. "Die Psychologische Bedeutung der Perspektive in Analysandenzeichnungen", Jung Institute Thesis, Zurich, 1975.

BUTLER, Christopher. *Number Symbolism in Europe,* London 1970.

CHALOUPKA, George. *Journey in Time: The 50,000-year Story of the Australian Aboriginal Rock Art of Arnhem Land*, Victoria 1993.

CHEVALIER, Jean and GHEERBRANT, Alain (eds). *Dictionnaire des symboles: mythes, rêves, coûtumes, gestes, formes, figures, couleurs, nombres*, Paris 1974.

CLOTTES, Jean and LEWIS-WILLIAMS, David. *Schamanen: Trance und Magie in der Höhlenkunst der Steinzeit*, Sigmaringen 1997.

EDELMAN, Gerald M. and TONONI, Giulio. *A Universe of Consciousness: How Matter becomes Imagination,* New York 2000.

EDWARDS, Betty. *Drawing on the Right Side of the Brain*, Los Angeles 1979.

EIBL-EIBESFELDT, Irenäus. *Human Ethology*, New York 1989.

ELIADE, Mircea. *Shamanism: Archaic techniques of ecstasy*, transl. from the French by Willard R. Trask. (Bollingen series 76), New York 1964.

ELKIN, Adophus Peter. *Aboriginal Men of High Degree: Initiation and Sorcery in the World's Oldest Tradition*, Sydney 1946, Rochester VT 1993.

ENDRES, Franz Carl and SCHIMMEL, Annemarie. *The Mystery of Numbers,* New York 1993.

FRANZ, Marie-Louise Von. *C.G. Jung: His Myth in our Time*, New York 1975.
- *Projection and Recollection in Jungian Psychology: Reflections of the*

- *Soul*, La Salle, London 1978.
- *Patterns of Creativity Mirrored in Creation Myths*, New York 1972.
- *Number and Time: Reflections Leading Towards a Unification of Psychology and Physics,* London 1978.
- *On Divination and Synchronicity: The Psychology of Meaningful Chance*, Toronto 1980.
- *Time, Rhythm and Response*, London 1978.
- *Individuation in Fairytales*, New York 1976.
- *Aurora Consurgens: A Document attributed to Thomas Aquinas on the Problem of Opposites in Alchemy*, Bollingen 1966.
- *Light from the Darkness: The Paintings of Peter Birkhäuser. Licht aus dem Dunkeln: Die Malerei von Peter Birkhäuser*. With contributions by Marie-Louise von Franz and Eva Wertenschlag, Basel, Boston, Berlin 1991.

FREUD, Sigmund. *The Interpretation of Dreams*. Authorised translation of 3rd German edition by A. A. Brill, London 1913.

FRICK, Karl R.H. (ed.). *Eröffnete Geheimnisse des Steins der Weisen oder Schatzkammer der Alchemie,* Graz 1976.

FURTH, Gregg. *The Secret World of Drawings. Healing through Art.* Boston 1988.

GERSHON, Michael D. *The Second Brain: The Scientific Basis of Gut Instinct and a Groundbreaking new Understanding of Nervous Disorders of the Stomach and Intestine.* New York, 1988.

HARTUNG VOM HOFF, Caspar. "Das Kunstbüchlein des Alchemisten Caspar Hartung vom Hoff", B. Haage (ed.), in: *Litterae—Göppinger Beiträge zur Textgeschichte*, U. Müller/F. Hundsnurscher/C. Sommer (eds.), Göttingen 1975. With comment by B. Haage.

HOPPER, Vincent Foster. *Medieval Number Symbolism*, New York, 1938.

HUETHER, Gerald. *Die Welt der inneren Bilder,* Göttingen 2004.

IBN UMAIL, Muḥammad. *Book of the Explanation of the Symbols. Kitāb Ḥall ar-Rumūz*, Th. Abt and W. Madelung (eds.), Corpus Alchemicum Arabicum (CALA 1), Zurich 2003.

ITTEN, Johannes. *Kunst der Farbe*, Studienausgabe, Ravensburg 1971.

JABIR Ibn Hayyan. Kutub al-mawazin. O. Houdas (ed.), in: M. Berthelot. *Histoire des sciences: La chimie au moyen âge*. Vol. 3, Paris 1893.

JACOBI, Jolande. *Vom Bilderreichtum der Seele*, Zurich 1963.

JUNG, Carl Gustav. *Psychological Types. Collected Works,* 6, Princeton 1974.
- *Structure and Dynamics of the Psyche. Collected Works,* 8, Princeton 1969.
- *The Archetypes and the Collective Unconscious. Collected Works,* 9/1, Princeton 1968.
- *Aion. Collected Works,* 9/2, Princeton 1968.
- "A Modern Myth of Things Seen in the Sky" in: *Civilization in*

Transition. Collected Works, 10, Princeton 1970.
- *Psychology and Alchemy. Collected Works*, 12, Princeton 1968.
- *Alchemical Studies. Collected Works*, 13, Princeton 1967.
- *Mysterium Coniunctionis. Collected Works*, 14, Princeton 1970.
- *The Symbolic Life. Collected Works*, 18, Princeton 1980.
- *Seminar über Kinderträume*, Eidgenössische Technische Hochschule, (Seminare, Zurich, 1938/39), Olten 1987.
- *Memories, Dreams, Reflections*, New York 1963.
- *Nietzsche's Zarathustra. Notes of the seminar given in 1934–1939.* J. L. Jarrett (ed.), Vol. I–II, Bollingen, Princeton 1988.
- and PAULI, Wolfgang. *Naturerklärung und Psyche*, Zurich 1952.

KELLOG, Rhoda. *Finger Painting in the Golden Gate Nursery School*, San Francisco 1951 (private printing).

KHANNA, Madhu. *Yantra: the Tantric Symbol of Cosmic Unity*, New York 1980.

KNAPP, Martin. *Pentagramma Veneris*, Basel 1934.

KOCH, Karl. *The Tree Test: The Tree-drawing Test as an Aid in Psychodiagnosis*, Berne 1952.
- *Der Baumtest. Der Baumzeichenversuch als Psychodiagnostisches Hilfsmittel*, Berne 1976.

KRÄTZ, Otto (ed.). *Goethe und die Naturwissenschaften*, München 1998 (2nd corrected edition, special edition).

LÜSCHER, Max. *The Lüscher colour test.* Based on the original German text by Max Lüscher. Ian A. Scott (translator and editor), London 1970.

MAIER, Michael. *Atalanta Fugiens*, Frankfurt 1618.
- *Symbola aurea mensa*, Frankfurt 1617.

MANGET, Johann J. (ed.). *Bibliotheca Chemica Curiosa*, 2 vols., Geneva 1702.

MARQUARDT, Hanna. *Reflexzonenarbeit am Fuss*, Heidelberg 1975.

MITTELSPACHER, Steffan. *Cabala: speculum artis et naturae, in alchymia*, Augsburg 1654.

MÜLLER, K. Alex. "Einiges zur Symmetrie und Symbolik der Zahl Fünf" in: H. Atmannspacher, H. Primas, E. Wertenschlag-Birkhäuser (eds). *Der Pauli-Jung-Dialog und seine Bedeutung für die moderne Wissenschaft*, Berlin, Heidelberg, New York 1995, pp. 275–294.

NETTESHEIM, Agrippa of. *Liber quartus de occulta philosophia*, 1565.

Museum Hermeticum, Frankfurt 1678.

Mutus Liber, La Rochelle 1677.

OVIDIUS NASO, Publius. *Metamorphoses,* Cambridge 2000.

PANETH, Ludwig. *Zahlensymbolik im Unbewusstsein*, Zurich 1952.

PAULI, Wolfgang and JUNG, Carl Gustav. *Atom and Archetype—the Pauli/Jung Letters, 1932–1958*, C.A. Meier (ed.), London 2001.

PRINZHORN, Hans. *Artistry of the Mentally Ill: A Contribution to the Psychology and Psychopathology of Configuration.* Translated by Eric von Brockdorff from the second German edition, with an introduction by James L. Foy, Vienna 1995, 1st edition Vienna 1972.

RENNERT, Helmut. *Merkmale schizophrener Bildnerei*, Jena 1962.

RENTSCH, Bernhard. *Neuere Probleme der Abstammungslehre*, 2nd ed. Zurich 1954.

RIEDEL, Ingrid. *Farben: In Religion, Gesellschaft, Kunst und Psychotherapie*. Stuttgart 1983.

SPECK, Frank. *Naskapi–The Savage Hunters of the Labrador Peninsula*, Oklahoma 1935, New Edition, Oklahoma 1977.

STOLTZIUS VON STOLTZENBERG, Daniel. *Viridarium chymicum* (dt. "Chymisches Lustgärtlein"), Frankfurt 1624. Reprint F. Weinhandl (ed.), Darmstadt 1987.

TINBERGEN, Niko. *The Study of Instinct*, Oxford 1951.

ULLMANN, Manfred. "Kleopatra in einer arabischen alchemistischen Disputation", in: *Wiener Zeitschrift für die Kunde des Morgenlandes*, Wien, Vol. 63/64 (1972).

WERTENSCHLAG-BIRKHÄUSER, Eva. *Fenster zur Ewigkeit:. Die Malerei von Peter Birkhäuser*, (Jungiana. Beiträge zur Psychologie von C.G. Jung, Reihe B, Band 7), Küsnacht 2001.

WILHELM, Richard (ed.). *I Ching: The Book of Changes*, Bollingen Series, Princeton University Press, New York 1950.

- *The Secret of the Golden Flower: a Chinese Book of Life*, translated [into German] by R. Wilhelm and explained, with a foreword and commentary by C.G. Jung. Translated into English by Cary F. Baynes. New and revised edn. London and New York 1962.

Index

- A -

Aborigines   22, 25, 168
Abt, T.   46, 88, 156
Abu al-Qāsim, M.   60
active imagination   174
Agrippa of Nettesheim   131–2, 138
air   46, 47, 130, 153, 174
albedo 104, 175
alchemy   9, 30–37, 40, 88, 91, 96, 97, 102, 104, 134, 145, 146–7, 152, 154, 160, 168, 175
Allendy, R.   123, 132, 134, 142
ambivalence   66, 118, 122
Amduat   88, 144, 156
amplification   28, 59, 60, 84, 122, 166
    circumambulation   46–51, 53, 55, 74, 174
    of numbers   111, 116–65
    personal associations   43, 48, 60
    pondering about pictures   29, 30, 41, 55
analytical work   12, 29, 30, 35–7, 53–60, 126, 168
anima   32, 161
animals   17, 20–1, 24, 34, 61, 64, 83, 90, 94, 119, 129
animus   141
anthropos   153
Apollo   150
Apophis   144
apostles   160
archaic identity   17

archetype/archetypal   26, 27–28, 35, 59, 61, 67, 76, 79, 91, 99, 108, 151
    —, of order (see also *day, month, year*)
aspective (see also *perspective*)   80–1
assimilation   35
association   59–60
    disciplined —   59
    free —   59
astrology   135, 141, 156–7
attitude (see also *consciousness*)
    extraversion —   41–43, 72, 74, 88
    introversion —   41–43, 74, 88
Atalanta fugiens   40
Aurora Consurgens   154
Australia   22, 25, 168

- B -

backbone   125
Bader, A.   169
ballpoint pen   65
Balzac   123
Beatrice   150
Bennet, E.A.   12
bipolarity (see also *one-continuum*)   97, 117
birds   16, 20, 24, 58, 101, 103, 122, 158, 171, 175
black   64, 70, 104–105, 119, 161

blue   92–3, 108, 167
body   84, 90, 97, 101, 121, 131
Book of Revelations   159
books of the afterlife (see *Amduat*)
border (boundary)   120, 128, 132, 164
brain   15, 17–19
bridges (bridging function)   30, 33, 114, 123, 162
brown   102–3
Brutsche, P.   80
Buddhism   35, 143, 147
Butler, C.   110, 152

- C -
C.G. Jung Institute   9, 10, 48, 52, 80, 100
Cartesian cross   127–29
causality (see also *thinking, synchronicity*)   111
cell, first living   50, 175
centring function (see also *order, chaos*)   74, 135, 158, 170
  lack of —   171
Chaloupka, G.   22
change (see also *evolution, dynamic, time*)
  circular —   140
  cyclical —   140
chaos   69, 148
Chauvet   14, 22
Chevalier, J.   149
child/children (see also *sun, new —, sun-child*)   25, 64, 69, 120, 123, 145, 160
Christ   147, 153, 160, 162

Christian tradition/Christianity   92, 97, 103, 115, 120, 127, 129, 132, 155, 160
circle (see also *time, rhythm*)   74–5, 85, 127, 138, 139, 143, 156–7, 165, 166–7
  — of sun   87, 139, 156–7
circular change (see also *change, rhythm*)   74, 127, 139, 140
circumambulation
  — with the functions   46–51, 53, 55, 74, 174
Clottes, J.   16
cobra (see also *snake*)   126–7
collective unconscious (see also *unconscious*)   11, 12, 26, 28
colour(s) (see also *complementary colours*)   84–108
  basic —   84–95
  circle of the —s   85–9, 100
  cold —s   88, 93, 100
  mixed —   96–101, 108
  names of — (see *black, blue, brown, green, grey, orange, pink, red, violet, white, yellow*)
  —s of the rainbow   85–8
  —ed pencil   62
  — spectrum   85–8, 92, 100
  non- —s   102–7
  warm —s   88, 90, 93, 96, 98, 100
colour symbolism   28, 84–108
colour test (see *test*)
compensation   49, 69
complementary colours   88, 96, 99, 101
completeness of the circle   143

complex   34, 41, 82, 107
  autonomous content   34-35, 69
  overwhelming content   70, 119, 148, 171
conception   149
coniunctio oppositorum (see also *union of opposites*)   100
consciousness   12, 15, 23, 28, 33, 44–5, 51, 67, 75, 114, 120–121, 123, 128, 140, 148, 150, 156–7, 162, 165, 174
  ego —   17, 21, 44, 69, 124
  opus contra naturam   36
cosmic
  — order   91, 147, 149
  — wheel   147, 149
cosmogony   150
cosmos   140, 141, 147–50, 160
creation (see also *consciousness, evolution, development*)   123, 138, 140, 152
creative process   138, 140, 143, 150, 158
cross   83, 127, 133, 142
crystal   27–8, 140
cyclical (see *change, circle*)

- D -
daemonic forces (see *devil*)
dangers of picture interpretation   42, 48–9, 52–3, 55
Dante Alighieri   143, 150
dark (darkness)   45, 79, 82, 95, 104, 147, 162
day   18, 88, 123, 127, 139, 156–8

death   104, 107
depression   70, 92, 95, 104, 125, 156, 158
development
  — of consciousness   44
  line of —   76–8, 123
devil   35, 83, 90, 95, 97, 98, 101, 104, 120, 155, 171
diamond body   135
Diana   150
differentiate/differentiated   62, 119, 150, 164
directional (see also *down, up*)   123
disconnection   167
discrimination   120
dissociation   33
Divina Comedia   143, 150
divination   110, 114
down   76, 109, 121, 124, 161
dreams (see also *visions*)   12, 25, 26, 32, 56, 59–61, 123, 125, 141, 150, 174, 175
  children's dreams   25
drive/drives (see also *instinct*)   20, 24, 36–7, 61, 83, 97, 101, 119, 161
duality   120–1, 133
dynamism   123, 149–51, 158–9, 160–1

- E -
earth   46, 55, 58, 68, 76–7, 95, 101, 102, 130, 141, 153, 154, 174
Edelman, G.M.   18
Edwards, B.   18

effects of pictures 33–7
egg 43, 93, 103, 167–8, 175
ego 12, 35, 69–71, 80, 82, 102, 104, 169–71
   unstable — 81–2, 169–71
   weak — 65, 67, 70, 81, 169–71
ego-consciousness (see *consciousness*)
Egypt 16, 66, 80, 81, 88, 139, 144, 156, 168
Eibl-Eibesfeldt, I. 25, 26
eight-aspect of the one 147
elements 127, 130, 141, 152, 153, 154, 174–5
   series of — 60
eleven-aspect of the one 155
Eliade, M. 25
Elkin, A.P. 25
emotion 29, 30, 53, 63, 64, 84, 129
emotional upheaval 109, 124, 129, 169–71
Endres, F.C. 109, 124, 153, 165
energy (see also *fire*) 23, 71, 73–4, 83, 90, 98, 104
eros 83, 109, 150
erotic dimension 119
eternity 148
ether 46
ethology
   human — 25–6
evil 143
evolution
   — of psyche 12
   — of psychic elements (see *development*)

evolutionary development 123, 141
Explanation of the Symbols — the Book of The — 88
expression
   modes of — 66–8
   spontaneous — 52, 61–3, 64, 65, 66, 115
extraversion 41–3, 88
eye-brow flash 26

- F -

fairy tales 53, 84, 154, 174, 175
fantasies 11, 33, 123, 141, 146
fate 123–6, 141, 147, 158, 160–1
fateful
   — number 123, 125, 143, 160
feeling (function) 44–7, 53, 79, 143
feminine principle 50–1, 73, 120, 124, 127, 142, 146, 149, 161
fences 69
fertility 142–3
fingers 131, 152, 163
finger paint 34, 64, 69
fire (see also *energy*) 46–7, 124, 130, 151, 153, 154, 168, 174
fish 151
five-aspect of the one 133
flow of life (see *life*) 62, 65, 66, 74, 96, 125
flower 83, 92, 132–7, 141, 147
   rose — 127, 132
folk belief 162
foot 132
formal aspects 69–75
format 28, 44, 46, 67, 71

Index

change of — 67–8, 79–80
horizontal — 68, 79, 128
landscape — 67–8, 72, 78
portrait — 67–8, 79
vertical — 68, 72, 128
four functions (see also *feeling, intuition, sensation, thinking*) 44–7, 53, 164–5, 174–5
— and consciousness 44, 164–5
inferior function 45
main function 45
four-aspect of the one 127, 164
fourteen-aspect of the one 162–3
frame 30, 33, 44, 51, 67, 72, 128
Franz, M.-L. von 10, 21, 44, 109, 110, 111–4, 128, 134, 155, 175
free will 21, 25
Freud, S. 11, 48, 59
Frick, K.R.H. 91
functions (see *four functions*)
future 74, 78

- G -

Ğābir ibn Hayyān (see *Ibn Hayyān*)
Gershon, M.D. 17
Gheerbrant, A. 149
god/godhead 35, 81, 88, 100, 118, 121, 138, 156–7
goddess (see also *love goddess*) 90, 127, 134
Goethe 42, 85–6
green 73, 88, 91, 96–7
grey 106
grid 64, 69, 79

growth 72–3, 143
Grünwald, M. 77–8

- H -

Haf Pakar 143
hand 21–2, 125, 131, 135, 136
Hartung vom Hoff, C. 36, 37
healing process 97, 125, 156
heavenly bodies (see *planets*)
Hermes 96–7
hexagram 138
Holy Ghost 149
homogeneity 169
Hopper, V.F. 149
horizon
high (see also *horizontal, vertical*) 68, 169
horizontal 68, 79, 128,
Hornung, E. 88, 156
human ethology 25–6
Hüther, G. 15
hybris 67, 143, 155, 160
hypothesis 47–50, 175
counter-hypothesis 47–9, 175

- I -

I Ching 110, 111, 114, 123, 139–40, 147
Ibn Hayyān, Ğ. 165, 175
Ibn Umail 46, 88, 175
image (see also *picture*) 15, 17, 18, 20–4, 29, 32, 35, 40, 110, 111, 114, 123, 140, 147, 165

individuation (see also *development*)   11, 118, 148, 154
infinity   116, 148
initiation   29, 143
ink   62
instinct (see also *drive*)   20–4, 25
introverted attitude (see *attitude, introversion*)   37, 41–3, 72, 74, 88
intuition (function)   44–7, 53
inversion   80
Ishtar   134
Isis   104
Itten, J.   89, 96

- J -

Jacobi, J.   9, 73, 109
Jesus   160, 162
Judas   160
Jung, C.G.   11, 15, 21, 25–32, 35, 42, 45, 52, 59–60, 100, 111, 113, 117, 124, 128, 140, 159, 175
Jung Institute, Zürich (see *C.G. Jung Institute*)
Jupiter   142

- K -

Ka   162
Kellog R.   69
Khanna, M.   148
king
— and queen   162
old —   154
Knapp, M.   135

Koch, K.   72, 76, 78
Krätz, O.   86

- L -

landscape (see *format*)
lapis, the   152
Lascaux   16
left   74, 76, 109
Leto   150
Lewis-Williams, D.   16
life   23, 74, 96, 107–8
flow of —   62, 66, 115
new —   50, 107
number of —   132
light   74, 79, 94, 101, 147, 162, 174
— part of space   79
new —   162
liminality   120
limit
— of counting (see also *border*)   165
lion   162–3
liquidification   46
location   76–80
love goddess   134
Ishtar   134
Venus   134
lucky number   55, 144
lumen naturae   54
Lüscher, M.   84

- M -

macrocosm   155
magic
— practices/effects   33, 35, 69, 100–11, 127
— square   163

magical-causal thinking (see also *thinking*)   110–11
magical-numerological speculation (see also *speculation*)   112
Maier, M.   40, 58
mandala   35, 69, 82, 105, 148, 158–9
Mangetus, J. J.   153
mania   35
Marquardt, H.   132
Mars   90, 98, 142
masculine principle   17, 124
massa confusa   102
matter   36–7, 61–8, 104, 113
material aspects (see also *medium*)   61–8
Mayans   110, 149, 150
meaning   29, 37, 44, 54, 60, 68, 114, 174
medicine
— man (see also *shaman*)   25
medium (see also *material aspects*)   44, 46, 62–6, 71
Mercury   106, 141–2, 161
method   54–5, 175
Michel, Rudolf   9
microcosm   155
Middle Ages   43, 80, 147–8, 149, 167
midlife crisis   115
Mithraism   143, 147
Mittelspacher, S.   146
mixed mode of expression   66
month   127, 139, 143, 160
moon   33, 35, 37, 78, 83, 94, 127, 130, 139, 141–4, 153, 160, 161, 162

moon goddess (see *goddess*, *Venus*, *Ishtar*)
motif/motifs   25, 53, 58, 60, 71, 114, 166–71
cut-off —   67, 171
mountain of bliss   147
movement   74–5
Müller, K. A.   132
multiple unity   152
multiplicatio   152
Muses, the   150
Museum Hermeticum   146
music   141, 144
Mysterium Coniunctionis (see also *opposites*)   23, 100, 144, 162
mythology   19, 25, 77, 81, 96, 116, 174, 175

- N -
Naskapi   26
nature   17, 72–3, 96–7, 104, 114–15, 125, 148, 166
nets   69
neurosis   29, 55, 121
newspaper   61
Newton, I.   84–5
night   18, 88, 108, 122, 127, 139, 153, 156–7
nigredo   104
nine-aspect of the one   150
Nizami   143
Noah's Ark   165
nona-essentia   149
number symbolism   109–65

number
- — and order   113–5
- — and symbolic nature   109–12
- — and time   111, 117, 128
- — quality of   109–15, 117
- — quantity of   109–12, 117, 144

number/numbers   54–5, 116–65
- — one   116–9
- — two   109, 120–2
- — three   118, 122, 123–7
- — four   127–31
- — five   131–7
- — six   78, 138–41, 143
- — seven   141–7
- — eight   147–8
- — nine   149–51
- — ten   90, 152–4
- — eleven   155
- — twelve   143, 156–9, 160
- — thirteen   143, 160–1, 162
- — fourteen   162–3, 164
- — fifteen   163–4
- — sixteen   164
- — seventeen   165
- holy —   152, 165
- lucky —   55, 144
- perfect —   138
- unlucky —   54, 110, 114, 144

- O -

objective criteria   56
objective psyche   10, 52, 65
octagon   148

Odin   150
oil paint   66
old king (see *king*)
one-continuum   117–18
opposites/union of opposites   23, 55, 58, 65, 82, 100, 123, 129, 130, 140, 144, 152, 162, 171
opus contra natura (see also *consciousness*)   36
orange   98–9, 101, 167
order   41, 67, 69–71, 92
- — and number   113–15, 129
organic matter
- — structures   132
organization (see also *chaos, frame*)   69–71
orientation   44, 128
oscillating lines (see also *rhythm*)   121–2
ouroborus   125
Ovid, N. P.   121

- P -

Paneth, L.   109
paper format (see *format*)
paper size (see *size*)
participation mystique   118
Pauli, W.   111, 113
Pauli-Jung—dialogue   111, 113
pen (see *pencil, ballpoint pen, mixed mode of expression*)
pencil (see also *coloured pencil*)   62–3, 66
pentagon   132, 134
pentagram   132, 134–5, 138
perception   17, 44, 56, 110

perspective   80–3
  aspective —   80–1
  central —   69, 81–2
  decreasing —   81–2
  light —   79, 82
  linear —   82
  no —   82
  rupture of/in —   82, 169–70
Pharaoh   88, 156, 162
picture (see also *image*)
picture interpretation (see also *dangers of*)   12, 41–5, 175
pink   108, 167
pitfalls (see *dangers of picture interpretation*)
Planck, Max   11
planets/heavenly bodies   78, 141–3, 145, 147–8
polarity   23, 109, 120, 122, 123
portrait (see *format*)
prime number   132, 141
Prinzhorn, H.   121, 169
prism   84–5, 88–9
proportion   44, 71–3
proto-psyche   113
psyche (see also *unconscious, proto-psyche*)   12, 15, 19, 22–4, 65, 93, 94, 135, 148, 169
  — regulatory system   12, 22–3, 135, 152
psychic transformation   24, 28, 68, 75, 91, 114
psychosis
  latent —   35, 82, 169–71
purgatory   143

purification of soul   143
Pythagoreans   152

- Q -

qualitative aspect (see *number, quality of*)
quality of number (see *number, quality of*)
quantitative aspect (see *number, quantity of*)
quantity of number (see *number, quantity of*)
questions
  asking the picture —   41–3, 47–51, 53
  five —   51
  — and attitude   42–3
quincunx   134
quinta essentia   50, 134–5, 165, 174
  — of the four   134, 149, 165
  — of the six   143
  — of the eight   149
  — of the ten   155
  — of the twelve   160
  — of the fourteen   164
  — of the sixteen   165
quintessence (see *quinta essentia*)

- R -

radius   138
rainbow   85–8
red   90–1, 104, 175
reflection   24, 30, 35, 120
reflex-zones   131

rejuvenation   96, 104
religion   74, 110
religious dimension of pictures   23, 30, 35
renewal   69, 75, 91, 94–7, 149, 156–7
Rentsch, B.   113
resistance   33
rhythm
   basic —   116, 143
   oscillating —   115, 121, 123, 133
   steady —   123
rhythmic configuration   118
Riedel, I.   84
right   74–6
rite d'entrée   29, 107
rock art   14–16, 21–2
Roman numbers   131
Rorschach Test   53
Rosaceae (see also *flowers*)   132
rubedo   104, 175
runes   150
rupture
   — in perspective   82, 169–70
   — in style   122, 169–70

- S -
Saturn   104, 142
scale   141
scarab   81, 156, 168
Schiller, F.   86
Schimmel, A.   109, 124, 165
schizophrenia   48, 67, 121
sea   151

Self   11, 12, 93, 129, 150, 152
sensation (function)   44–7, 53
seven-aspect of the one   143–4
seventeen-aspect of the one   165
sex   24, 90, 138
sexual organ   138, 166
shadow (see also *dangers of picture interpretation*)   52, 82
shaman   25, 143
shamanistic initiations (see also *initiation*)   143
sheet   61, 76–7, 119
sickness   35
signal colour   90, 98
sin   155, 160
six-aspect of the one   139
sixteen-aspect of the one   164
size of paper   67, 71–2
snake   65, 82, 97, 106, 125, 126–7, 144, 158, 174
solar time   81, 156–7
soul   52, 63, 78, 147–8
soul-guide   150
space symbolism (see also *left*, *right*, *dark*, *light*)   44, 72, 76–83, 169–71
Speck, F.G.   26
spectrum   85
speculation   53
   magical-numerological   111–12
Sperry, R.W.   18
spiral   141, 166
spirit, spiritual   16, 21–2, 25, 26, 30, 55, 68, 72, 90, 92, 100–1, 113, 122, 144–45, 150, 152, 156–7, 161

Splendour Solis   91
split (see also *polarity*)   73, 119, 120–1
spontaneous expression (see *expression*)
square   68, 163
standpoint
   firm — (see also *ego, order, perspective*)   169
   lack of —   169
star(s)   35, 94, 147, 151, 161
   five-petalled —   133
steps   141
   seven —   141, 143, 145, 146, 148
Stoltzius von Stoltzenberg, D.   154, 160, 162
Stone of the Sages   104, 108, 134, 152
structure
   eightfold —   148
   fourfold —   127–8, 130, 158
   inorganic —   132
style
   — rupture (see *rupture in style*)
subconscious (see also *Freud, unconscious*)   6, 48
subtle body   135
sun   33, 35, 37, 51, 76, 78, 87–8, 91, 94–5, 115, 130, 141, 156–7
   new —   160, 162
   two —s   115
sun-child   145, 160
supervision groups   60
symbol   27–8, 33, 59, 61, 74, 83, 110, 123, 152, 174

symbolic nature
   — of numbers   109–65
symmetry   69, 117, 120, 122, 127, 133, 147, 153, 155, 164
synchronicity (see also *causality*)   111
synthesis   54–6

- T -
Tao   140, 155
Tantric yoga   74, 143
temperament(s)   86
ten-aspect of the one   153
tension, of opposites   23, 82, 123
tests
   colour —   28, 84
   tree —   28, 72–3, 99
Tetraktys   152
thinking (function)   17, 18, 44–7, 53
   causal —   111
   linear —   17, 18, 19
   magical-causal —   111–12
thirteen-aspect of the one   160
Thot   16, 96
three-aspect of the one   117
time   117, 123
   completion of — (*year, day,* see also *circle*)   123, 127, 139, 143
   unfolding —   139
Tinbergen, N.   20
toilet paper   61, 121
Tononi, G.   18
transformation   68, 75, 114, 143

tree   72–3, 76–7, 81, 130–1, 160, 174
tree test (see *tests*)
triangle   103, 123–4, 152, 166–7
trinity   103, 124
twelve-aspect of the one   156
two-aspect of the one   120, 123
typology (see also *attitude, four functions, extravert, introvert*)   41, 44–7, 86

- U -
Ullmann, M.   175
unconscious (see also *soul*)   11, 12, 19, 29–33, 44, 49, 50, 69–72, 74, 93, 96, 99, 110, 112, 169, 174
(see also *collective unconscious, inner world, lumen naturae, objective psyche*)
— background   16, 28, 114
— processes (see also *psychic regulatory system*)   12, 18, 22–3, 135, 152
union of creator and creation   138
— of heaven and earth   133, 138, 159
— of opposites   33, 55, 125, 129, 130, 133, 159, 162
uniqueness   118, 119, 135
uniting
— principle   148
— symbol   36, 83, 122–4
unity   54, 118, 152
unlucky numbers   54, 110, 114, 144

unus mundus   12
up   76, 109, 121, 124, 161

- V -
value system   61
  split —   115
vaporization   46
vegetation   96–7, 102, 157
Venus   90, 134–5, 142
vertical   68, 72, 128
vessel   35, 148, 168
violet   55, 88, 100–1
virgin-number   141
visions   11, 123, 125
Vita Nuova   150
von Franz, M.-L. (see *Franz*)

- W -
warm (see *colour(s)*)
water   46, 93, 124, 130, 140, 153, 154, 174
—colour   65, 66, 93, 103, 105, 119
—s of baptism   148
week   127, 141–3
wheel   147, 158
  eight-fold —   147
  four-fold —   158
  medicine —   147
  — of Buddhism   147
white   96, 104, 107, 136
wholeness   54, 106, 118, 124, 130, 154, 155
Wilhelm, R.   110

- Y -
year   127, 139, 156–7, 160
yellow   75, 88, 94–5, 101, 122, 161
Yang (see *Ying and yang*)
Ying and yang   120, 123, 150
yoni   124
Yoga   74, 143, 148

- Z -
zodiac   156, 158, 160

Sources of the Pictures

(The numbers are the figure numbers.)

G. Chaloupka 8

I. Eibl-Eibesfeldt 11

J. Jacobi 51, 77

C. G. Jung Heirs 12, 114

United Exhibits Group (Denmark) 2, 3, 4, 9

All other pictures by the kind permission of clients of the author.

All graphics are copyright of the author.